heart of gold

Books by Paul Williams

Outlaw Blues
Pushing Upward
Time Between
Das Energi
Apple Bay, or Life on the Planet
Right to Pass
Coming
Dylan — What Happened?
The Book of Houses (with Robert Cole)
The International Bill of Human Rights (editor)
Common Sense
Waking Up Together
Only Apparently Real: The World of Philip K. Dick
Remember Your Essence
The Map, or Rediscovering Rock and Roll
Performing Artist: The Music of Bob Dylan
Nation of Lawyers

heart of gold

a book by paul williams

ENTWHISTLE BOOKS

Heart of Gold

© 1991 by Paul Williams

cover painting © 1991 by Paula J. McCreary

Heart of Gold designed and set by Andy Watson

originally published by WCS Books, Englewood, Colorado

Library of Congress Cataloging in-Publication Data
Williams, Paul, 1948-
: ISBN 0-934558-37-X : $10.00
    1. Williams, Paul, 1948- 2. Journalists—United States—
Biography. 3. Authors, American—20th century—Biography.
I. Title.
PN4874/.W627A3   1991
070'.92—dc 20
[B]   91-24670

available from Ingram Book Co., or:

> Entwhistle Books
> Box 232517
> Encinitas CA 92023

and from: www.cdaddy.com

introduction

Can't introduce this book. Can't explain it.
For almost eighteen years people have
looked at *Das Energi* and asked me, "What's
it about?" and I still don't have an answer.
This one, I know what it's about — the
stories of our lives, what do you see when
you look in the mirror of the past, heart's
mirror? — but I've got another problem.
Don't know what it *is*.

It's not a story. It's about what it feels
like when I try to tell my story. Another
little piece of my heart. I wrote it with the
notion that everybody out there is trying to
tell a story every time you look into another
person's eyes.

And very few of us ever know that we

do sometimes, despite all the chaos and incompleteness, succeed a little bit in saying something, that in our lives we do actually get seen sometimes in our most naked beauty by friends, by other people.

The friends don't know how to tell us, or they do tell us and we don't know we've heard, and we go on believing we're so utterly alone. But it isn't completely true.

Heart of Gold is a cry from beyond the grave of love and utter astonishment at the fact of living and the news that we sometimes are in the same world as our other selves, and at the same time. Part one was written in short installments for a weekly newspaper in New York, and part two for another paper in Santa Cruz two years later. It was always intended to be a book, and now it is.

Paul Williams
Glen Ellen, California
February 1991

heart of gold

for Robin & Donna

I've been in my mind
It's such a fine line
That keeps me searching for a heart of gold
And I'm getting old.

— Neil Young

Hearts of gold are everywhere, hoping to find
each other.

— from an earlier draft of this manuscript

part one

I.

Well, I have always wanted to write about
my past, to conjure up the magic. When I
was in the sixth grade, I wrote a weekend
paper about the wild, special things we
used to do back in my fifth grade days. And
I wanted to write, and planned in my head,
a book, title now lost to me, which would
have been the story of both those years,
incredible sense of community in a small
experimental school in Cambridge, nine of
us in fifth grade I think and about fourteen
in sixth, co-ed, we lived intensely, loving,
fighting, writing & performing plays, fierce
friendships, cliques, conflicts, adventures
of every sort. We were adults unto ourselves at that time, whatever we may have

seemed to outsiders; we were up to our
eyeballs in human interrelations, our hearts
could be broken, our actions were all in
earnest & we had a lot of fun. And I did
even then feel the urge to preserve it somehow, a little bit of the essence & wonder of
it all . . .

High school days are closer to feeling
continuous with the present, so it's less of a
surprise to me to remember the stuff I
wanted to record then, in particular a book
(started thinking about this as early as
ninth grade anyway) called *The World Is
Crazy!* which would record the process of a
young man's discovery of that fact . . . I
mean, the things we found out, day by day
and month by month, about what was really
going on. Again, mostly relating to human
relations, sex, appearances and realities . . .
that sense of discovery, recognizing with
fear and awe the craziness of it all and how
it's the opposite of what they say, and
maybe finding one friend to share that
growing awareness with . . . it was a story, it
had to be told, because, uh, well because it
felt like it would feel good to tell it, to get it
down, somehow I dreamed of satisfaction in
that.

And still do.

In sixth grade, 1959, our favorite records were things like "Stagger Lee," by Lloyd

                                  Paul Williams

Price: "The night was clare, and the moon
was yellow, and the leaves came tumbling
down . . . " But there were things I personally got off on even more, specifically a 45
(of course) rpm record by Johnny & the
Hurricanes called "Crossfire." An instrumen-
tal, it buzzed through my mind with a drive
all its own that at moments seemed to carry
me away with it: I remember walking into
the library at school, which was also the
room where the plays were held, we were
rehearsing for something, possibly "The
Wind in the Willows" (a major event in my
life — I was Mole, in the dramatization
called "Toad of Toad Hall"; I had the first
line of the play, "This is fine! This is better
than whitewashing!") . . . I remember looking up at the stage, with "Crossfire" pound-
ing in my head, and experiencing some sort
of epiphany. I just knew at that moment
that everything I was, which was a lot,
which was the potential energy of a boulder
rolling down a mountain, invincible and
profound, was expressed in that bit of music, I just felt it all at once and the awe and
joy of that moment have stayed in my
memory since. I can still play the song in
my head, and understand.

I used to have all sorts of relics, papers, relating to these years in my life:
social studies reports from the third grade

and the dittoed newspaper I used to put
out, short stories by me and my friends
from sixth grade, poems, letters, programs
from the plays, notes passed in French
class in junior high school and correspon-
dence with science fiction fans and girl-
friends . . . I preserved this stuff, keeping it
in a box in my room and sorting through it
every few years, cutting the quantity in
half, keeping what was important, even
when I left home, left college, even when I
left the East and moved to California, in fact
I built an extraordinarily solid bed, Taurus
manifestation, with room underneath to
store my stuff securely (like a little cave,
you could crawl in); but then when I left
California and went to Canada there was
just too much essential stuff to carry and I
let my personal things travel in the other
vehicle, Alan would be right behind us in
the truck in a day or two . . . Yeah he never
came, and all those boxes of stuff, the ones
left after 90% was given or thrown away,
stayed behind when he moved a few miles
away, and eventually the new owners took
them to the dump and burned them —
yeah, the box with the special relics too. I
was far away and forced to be cool about
the whole thing, but clearly I still feel the
loss. Appreciate it, see the rightness in it,
but feel it.

                                      Paul Williams

It made me glad that I'd taken most of what I most wanted made public and put it in a book some months before leaving California . . . as if I knew that whatever didn't get published, get into book form and out of my hands, would fall over a cliff someday. So I miss the private things but really it was all *aide-memoire*, most of what I would have wanted anyone else to see I'd already rescued.

Which brings me back to my starting thought, writing about the past. I'm experimenting with music as a touchstone. My letters are a fabulous *aide-memoire* now lost to me short of some sort of extraordinary hypnosis, but phonograph records are public, like books; and though I gave away all my precious ones over the years of travelling and shedding possessions, the records can still be obtained again, heard again, and that part of the feeling sometimes somewhat released.

It's like a piece of the personal stored in a public place . . . yeah, many of the records are out of print and so one haunts the oldies shops and makes deals and makes cassettes and sometimes pays high prices, but it's all there somewhere, the problem of getting it to sound the way it did once, on the cheap equipment and all, that can be tricky too (those few times that

it matters) but perfectly possible, it's all
within reach.

As for why go back, it isn't that, there's
no way to do that, it's just what's here right
now. All this stuff is inside, and all I know
is the next step is letting it show.

Set the heart free by letting it speak.

Can you see me?

Paul Williams

II.

The voyage to maturity takes seven years —
at least, it did in my case — or anyway I'm
saying it did for the sake of structuring this
story. I left my childhood in 1965, frightened and hungry. The Rolling Stones knew
what I was going through: they released
"(I Can't Get No) Satisfaction" two weeks
before I graduated from high school.

I arrived at my adulthood, or some sort
of resting place, in 1972. My arrival, like my
departure, was accompanied by music: an
album called *Harvest*, written and per-
formed by Neil Young. There was a song on
that album called "(Searching For A) Heart
of Gold." The song's title became the title of
a record review that I wrote early in 1972

for a Japanese music magazine:

> That heart of gold he's searching
> for — that heart of gold *I'm*
> searching for — that h. of g. you're
> looking for — it's not some other
> person. It's me — it's you — it's
> Neil Young — it's the heart of gold
> inside. The untapped vein. I know
> it's here somewhere.

The essay that followed that first paragraph was as much a review of my own life as an appraisal of Neil Young's album. "Heart of Gold" was and is a real touchstone for events in my life starting around November 1971, when I first heard the song (and recorded it on my cassette-recorder).

Everywhere I went for the next four months, up and down the West Coast of America and then over to Japan, I played the song for people who'd never heard it before, and they were invariably moved. In the great tradition, it was a totally personal, totally universal, anthem-of-the-moment.

> It's all about men and women.
> Right on. It's the only story I know,
> the broken heart, don't try to sell
> me no mystic enlightenment. Will I
> only harvest some? Yeah, but a

little more each year. Deeper sor-
row and greater joy. And there's no
turning back. I've been loving you
too long to stop now.
   This album is about the pain of
becoming increasingly conscious.
It's about how hard it is to be loved.

I had been on a long lonely trip, not
that different from anyone else's lonely trip
I'm sure, and I found great comfort in
hearing someone sing about a similar
experience. My trip had taken me from
Cambridge, Mass. to New York City to the
forests of Northern California to the iso-
lated coastline of western Canada back to
New York and Boston and then finally back
again to the West Coast and on to Tokyo by
freighter, great symbolic ocean crossing, I'd
chased my shadow and been chased by my
shadow all over hell and back and now it
seemed I'd washed up on shore at last,
gasping for breath, amazed at the whole
relentless sequence of events and just
happy to be alive and on solid ground.

   . . . And the fine line that keeps
   us searching is ultimately what I
   want to call your attention to, it's
   the line between good and evil, the
   line between sky and sea, the thin

edge on which we walk over the
infinite, belief in ourselves, it's
the fine line of faith in the face
of doubt, god bless us all who
continue to dare to love.

Shortly after completing my "review,"
my diary entry, I met my future mate and
right away we conceived our first child, just
starting all over again. That story is still in
progress. This book, this essay, is the story
of what came before.

Paul Williams

III.

Under the moon, on a cold spring night, it all comes back. I remember why I was so drawn to the blues, to the white blues singers (all six of them), why I even wrote blues songs myself and sang them to myself standing alone on the street on late nights like this.

It was the romanticism I hungered for (and rightly so); in the words sung and feelings expressed I saw/felt a romantic vision that encompassed my own life and feelings, that I could be part of, that I could believe in, nothing corny or out-of-date like Rod McKuen or Sir Walter Scott. I could hear the soul, the real, in Dave Ray, Dave Van Ronk, Eric Von Schmidt, I could hear it and I loved

it, those voices and guitars (add: Geoff
Muldaur, John Koerner) woke up the sleeping cosmic tuning fork inside me and set it
vibrating fiercely.

Songs of sex, of loneliness, of friendship, of travel, hard times and good times,
it all let me know that I wanted more than
anything to become a romantic figure *to
myself*, I wanted to be able to view my life
critically and dig the rhythm of what I saw.
Wanted to hear that strong solid blues guitar on my personal soundtrack, and no
bullshit, the real thing.

> Last bus
> Last bus
> Last bus out of town
> If I don't catch that old last bus
> I'll just keep walking on down . . .

I never wrote any verses to this song
that I can remember (the tune's some vari-
ation on "Erie Canal," perhaps) but it's a
good case in point because when I hear it in
my head now it evokes the scene, the way I
felt the air around me and dug the privacy,
of me standing on Concord Avenue in Cambridge at age sixteen not far from my girlfriend's house waiting for the last bus out
of Harvard Square (12:26 a.m.) or starting to
walk home five miles because I'd already

missed it. Good feeling, not the fact of the situation but the quietness of the street at that hour, the way the scene spoke for my personal world because it was after all my creation, the product of my needs, my private madness, my actions. No one else standing there doing the same thing.

My place. Music as one of the tools by which we take possession of the planet.

And what I heard in Dave Ray singing/playing Leadbelly ("This fore-day worry blues done got down on me . . . ") was of course Leadbelly but it was also the passion with which Ray felt and expressed Leadbelly or whatever he heard in Leadbelly, which made it Ray, which brought it into my present you see, not just digging on some ago black singer but digging on the now uprooted-white-guy-like-me digging him. Not an intellectual move mind you (Cambridge a real cesspool of intellectualized culture), I just dug Dave Ray a whole hell of a lot and didn't quite get the same buzz off the Leadbelly records I heard and didn't worry about it much.

Because I mean it was a private thing so I could just rejoice at my good fortune at actually *hearing* something, you know, with every bone in my body, and not have to sweat the aesthetics of it.

Of course I had my head screwed up in

other ways and resisted rock 'n' roll as long
as I could but that's another story, today's
story is like me in 1965 giving a girl I had a
crush on a copy of the new Dave Ray album
Snaker's Here! for Valentine's Day because I
just wanted to buy another copy (very big
expenditure at the time) and give it to
someone with all of my heart, so *much* a
piece of me, as satisfying as anything else I
might have done with her.

And out of all the great songs on
Snaker's Here! (each a masterpiece with
which I was more than intimate — worlds
unfolded for me, I'd never heard such pure
spirit), the one that most penetrated my
soul, especially those first few months
when I was wearing the album flat, was
"Rock Me," third song first side, Ray and
Glover (Tony "Little Sun" Glover on
harmonica)'s version of Muddy Waters'
"I Just Want to Make Love to You."

Sex. The song was total sensuality,
male, me, maybe you could say the song
made love to me but I felt it was me talking
to whomever. Harmonica apotheosis. I even
tried to learn how to play. It was magnificent, it was so much pleasure, it was in fact
the sound of me making love to someone,
the sound of the feeling. Mm.

And the thing is, I was sixteen, I was
horny, I was in love, but I was a virgin,

unexperienced, it hadn't happened yet, and
of course I wonder what part that played in
my relationship to the music. Some sort of
release of tension? Or maybe it was the
existence of that tension that made me such
a great receptive ear.

No simple answers, please. I came out
of the sleepwalking society of Cambridge a
very awake and happily hungry adolescent,
and I want to thank those guitar players for
doing their part.

IV.

"Baby I feel good / from the moment I
rise . . . " Listening to "Till the End of the
Day" I feel, suddenly, a desire to call *Kinks
Kontroversy* one of the few truly great rock
albums, an expression of the times, or some
such claptrap. Why? Where on earth — years
after I've stopped writing about rock music,
almost stopped listening to it altogether —
did that urge come from?

I asked myself that question and the answer so startled me in its simplicity that I
thought I'd try to write it down for old times'
sake. Here goes: the desire to call a record
(or book or painting or place or time or
person) "great" (or "good" or "bad" or anything) is the desire to say, "I am," "I exist."

I want to tell you how much I like this record, how wonderful *Kinks Kontroversy* sounds to me at this moment, because this delight I feel is the very essence of myself, it feels so good, I want to spread it around. I want to express my self.

There is only one statement, and it is: I am. You say who you are by saying what you perceive. Your time/space coordinates (personal perspective) (nervous system) is/are unique, and you define you (express your uniqueness) by saying how it looks from where you are.

If I could fully tell you how this Kinks record makes me feel, you would know completely who where what I am, my situation, location, you would know me, you would BE me.

You are.

I'm twenty-seven years old. For a number of years I felt a rather strong sense of identification with other members of my generation. It was an exuberant feeling, much of the time. But these days . . . well, no complaints, it's just different. I'm in some sort of null-zone; not at odds with my generation, just a lot less sure of who it is and what we're doing. I know what *I'm* doing, thanks; but for better or worse I'm no longer so full of ideas about how it fits

                                    Paul Williams

with what everyone else it up to. Lost sight of the fleet, so I'm just sailing by the seat of my pants.

I exist. Listening to certain beloved albums (on the stereo or in my head) returns me at different moments to many different worlds within worlds. For example, I can remember what I would call the *texture* of what I felt the first twenty or thirty times I heard the Kinks' song "Come On Now." It was the spring of 1965.

What did I feel? I guess it was a new kind of communication: I got a personal message (reflection of myself) from the song, but of a different kind than what I'd been hearing in Van Ronk and Dave Ray. The Rolling Stones were not so different from what I'd been listening to — white guys playing the blues, full of awareness of and respect for the great country blues singers and Chicago bluesmen. But the Kinks, though they were also into American black music, were something else; they were pop, like the Beatles; by no extension of the imagination could they be called a blues band. Yet I liked them.

("Come on now while we've still got time/ Come on baby the sun is shining / Put on your coat and stop your whining.")

That peculiar, appealing voice (not just the accent but the attitude), the equally odd harmonies, very special chukka-chukka rhythm-guitar-and-bass sound, all nicely-structured, self-contained despite incredible brevity . . . it worked for me, connected and contrasted nicely with the "rough-sounding" "All Day And All Night" which, along with "You Really Got Me," originally attracted me to the Kinks. (I heard that sound on the radio in the Senior Room in high school and was immediately interested, attentive, although I believed I couldn't stand rock and roll.)

These songs and their albums weren't played much at the parties I went to; they were to some extent a peculiar discovery of my own. I didn't rate the Kinks quite as super-high as the Stones or Dave Ray, but they were important to me. I felt very close to their music.

a) The Kinks. b) Who I was in 1965, and what was happening to me. c) How music communicates. d) The stories of our lives.

The stories of our lives have no beginning and no end. In 1968, on an acid trip (listening to *Anthem of the Sun* by the Grateful Dead and Beethoven piano concertoes played by Lily Kraus), a friend of mine nailed me: "You writers pretend that things all come together and climax at a particular time and place, you create all this anxiety around a single, significant moment, which you have to do to tell a story I guess, but which really isn't the way things are." (He was berating me for encouraging his wife's tendency towards melodrama. Psychedelics bring out the hysteric in me, no question about it.)

The stories of our lives are different from our current opinions of newspaper events, or from the things we say when asked who we are. "I grew up in the suburbs of Boston, Mass . . . I work as a freelance writer." No. The stories of our lives roll like hoops across the landscape, a whole bunch of them at once, going in different directions. The stories of our lives lie like paper clips in a drawer, lost, forgotten, waiting to be used for something.

And while I'm writing this I'm playing "You Really Got Me" over and over again in my mind.

In 1965 I was in turmoil. Love turmoil, sex turmoil, freedom turmoil — great stuff, at least in retrospect. But agony. My heart was open, and lots of things happened to it. And in making the transition from hard-working high school student to whatever came next (naturally I thought college but it didn't finally work out that way) I lost the rhythm of my life, lost the meaning, my day-to-day motivating force, everything

changed around and I couldn't get a hold on
it at all. And I was in love, constantly in
love. It was a hell of a year.

The music was incredible. Dave Ray.
Françoise Hardy. The Rolling Stones (*Now*,
"Satisfaction"). "Ticket To Ride." Von
Schmidt. Richard & Mimi Fariña. The Kinks.
The Yardbirds. Them. "Subterranean Home-
sick Blues." "Mr. Tambourine Man." "Like A
Rolling Stone." The Beau Brummels. Paul
Butterfield. The Lovin' Spoonful. The Hol-
lies. Sonny Boy Williamson. "Hang On
Sloopy." "Daytripper." *Rubber Soul.*

It was a year for feeling, not achieving.
But for that very reason, it is nobler in my
memory than the achievement years that
followed. Of course, every year has its own
dignity. At any rate, without the occasional,
explosive years of feeling, the achievement
years would not be possible.

I believed my ears. And every new wonder I heard just took me further away from
the straight and narrow, led me deeper into
the wilderness.

"Girl, you really got me now, you got
me so I don't know what I'm doing . . ."

V.

My name is Don McNeill. I've been dead almost
seven years now. You might think that gives me a
certain distance, perspective, but it's not quite like
that. I'm free, that's all; I'm free of measured time.
I'm out of my body, yes; but more important, I'm
out of chronology. When I died, I became discon-
tinuous, invisible to your eyes; but I never lost
consciousness. Can you believe that?

It doesn't matter. I want to tell you a story,
about my friend Paul: how I met him, some things
he told me on our acid trips, some things he
didn't tell me, some things he doesn't know.

When I met Paul he was eighteen years old;
I was twenty-two. I was a reporter for *The Village
Voice*; and I first met Paul, briefly, in connection
with the Easter Be-In (Central Park, 1967), which

he and Jim Fouratt helped organize. Fouratt was a mutual friend and he introduced us. We spoke for a minute or two, in my office at Sheridan Square. But Jim quickly dominated the conversation, as he tended to in those days, and so the meeting was a superficial one. I don't know if Paul would even remember it.

We met more permanently about a month later, at a place called Pablo, a storefront on Bleecker two doors from the Bowery. Some sort of gathering had been scheduled, one of the endless, fruitless gatherings that spring, tribal community "leaders" trying to work together to plan for the summer influx of kids and energy. People came, words were spoken, things drifted apart inconclusively. Paul and I started talking in a corner of the room, and the conversation was so enjoyable we continued it after the meeting broke up, shifting the scene to my loft a block away.

We took some acid, and talked all night.

Something in Paul — his youth, his energy, his intelligence — was very attractive to me. There was an easy intimacy in our conversation, a quality of mutual relaxation, right from the beginning. We became close friends. That acid trip was the first of many we took together . . . always unplanned, almost always starting in my Bleecker Street loft.

Thirty minutes into the trip Paul would collapse, every time. Sometimes he would hide his fear as best he could, slipping into the bathroom to be alone, riding the storm, reemerging after a cathartic session on the crapper. Other times he would turn to me for help, terrified, trembling, I'd talk him through, anything I could think of to involve his mind and get him past the rush — this long-haired, wild-eyed, skinny, slightly pimply teenage whiz kid, so vulnerable, so completely trusting, so finely-tuned to my own thoughts and needs . . . He became a very special friend to me, there are no other words to describe the warmth of that chaste relationship. We were fellow travelers in the psychedelic night, and our visions always meshed.

He was two years out of high school, editing a magazine he'd started himself, *Crawdaddy!*, "the magazine of rock"; I was a musical ignoramus when I met Paul, and had never seen the magazine, but his enthusiasm for the music and for his writers was irresistible — I became a convert. We walked to the *Crawdaddy!* office, Third Street and Sixth Avenue, just before sunrise, that first trip, and he played me a record by Country Joe and the Fish that was unlike anything I'd ever heard before. I saw the dawn in that music, heard the sun rise out of the silence. It was one of the great ecstatic moments of my life.

My friend was nervous, he loved to talk — full of ideas, full of thoughts that connected to other thoughts, explanations of the details of the universe, made up on the spur of the moment, miraculous world without end. I would look at him sometimes and wonder where he came from. My own Pacific Northwest roots left me completely unable to imagine an East Coast childhood — for me, East Coast meant adulthood, post-adolescence, the magical, mystifying world I entered the day I first set foot in New York City.

Paul dropped by in the afternoon, the day after our first trip together. I was cleaning some grass; we got pretty stoned. A couple of other people were there, and Paul seemed to withdraw from the scene. I found him lying on my bed in the other room, he was pretty spaced — face full of fear, and asking for downers. I didn't have any, but I gave him a bourbon and water. He asked me to play "Sad-Eyed Lady" from *Blonde on Blonde*, then rejected that after the first minute and switched to *Between the Buttons*.

I figured he'd pull through it okay, but I gave him my full attention, because — well, that seemed to be what he wanted. I held his hand and he started talking, trying to explain something to me — something about climbing mountains, and how we were both reporters . . . it made perfect sense at the time.

The more he talked the more excited he got, in a good way; his involvement in what he was telling me was taking him away from that scary place, that vision that had so terrorized him a few minutes earlier. He sat forward suddenly, to express himself better, and I knew at that moment he was out of it. His eyes were alive again. He kept on explaining, jumping ahead and then falling back, in his roundabout way, every digression ultimately accounted for, pulling me inexorably towards the heart of his particular darkness.

Paul told me about his childhood. He learned to read very young. As a result, he was ahead of his classmates in first grade, and grew very restless. After two months he was allowed to "skip a year" and become a second grader. It was a good change: he became involved in his schoolwork, and found a close friend in that second grade class. But for the rest of his school career (right through his first and only year of college) he was a year younger than most of the people around him.

His mother moved him from the local public school to a small private school a bus ride away, starting in the fifth grade. It was an experimental school attached to a teachers' college; Paul's class that first year contained nine people. The personal attention, the friendliness of the environment were liberating experiences for a kid who got Ds in public school because of poor penmanship, who by his own account used to follow his "friends" around from house to house, on foot and by bicycle, while they did their best to lose him.

(He had been to a child psychiatrist at some point in his grammar school years. He never said much about this, but it seemed to be a particularly bitter memory. I don't know what sort of problem was being dealt with, or why Paul disliked the

experience so much. My guess is that his mother
was worried by his lack of friends; and that he
resented this intrusion into an already delicate,
painful part of his life.)

Fifth grade and sixth grade were idyllic, as he
recalled them to me. He came alive, found friends,
found a sense of himself that he could feel comfortable with. And then, because that school
ended with the sixth grade, he entered a tradi-
tional private day school, moving from a coeducational class of fourteen students to an all-male
class of about fifty.

The roof fell in again. At Browne & Nichols,
boys were addressed by their family names, and it
happened that year there were two Williamses. For
the purpose of making announcements, these two
boys were identified by their surnames *plus* first
initials. So it was natural enough for the headmaster of the Middle School (grades 7 through 9) to
get up at lunch one day in the fall of Paul's first
year and conclude the daily list of punishments
(for talking in study hall and what-have-you) with
this request: "I would like to see Williams, P. after
lunch."

A considerable part of the lunchroom crowd
(the entire Middle School) spotted the pun at
once, and broke into laughter. The others, including Paul, were made wise soon enough. And Paul,
though as the eldest of three brothers he was
perfectly accustomed to dishing it out, was not
very good at taking teasing — and of course the

Paul Williams

more you squirm and respond and get angry, the more you get teased. Paul — "Pee," "Peewee" — became the class chump, the butt of all jokes that year, or at least enough to keep him constantly miserable.

He almost left the school that spring, held back by only two things: his fear of the new school he was considering as an alternative (he somehow found out that one of the teachers there had argued against his admittance), and the conversation he'd had with a member of the B&N faculty who'd sought him out and urged him not to leave B&N, in particular because he, this faculty member, wanted Paul to try out for the wrestling team next winter. That conversation tipped the balance. Paul stayed in the place where, despite all his problems, he felt more wanted.

And did become a wrestler, as well as a star English student, a writer for the school newspaper and literary magazine, and a heavily-involved member of the dramatics club. He stage-managed two major productions, acted — clumsily, he says — in a third, and eventually was voted club president, the closest he ever came to winning a popularity contest.

But that was years later, four and a half years later. The jokes about Williams peeing disappeared after a while, but the shyness that originally encouraged those jokes — a kind of arrogant shyness, the kid who knows all the answers in class but is unable to hang out and talk with you afterwards — dissolved only very gradually, and only to a point. Paul was at times outgoing during the months we spent together, but he was never really social. He had no knack for putting strangers at their ease. This made it hard for him to get to know people.

And at the same time his need for people, for real intimate human interaction with people, was very strong.

His parents fought continuously starting when he was about four until they separated for the last, final time when he was nine years old. He and his brothers lived with their mother, who worked during the day, then came home and made dinner, and who balanced her saint-like strength with an unfortunate bad temper. She would become enraged at seemingly small incidents, and her fury fed on itself, often lasting many hours, while the three boys, depending on their temperaments, defended themselves, withdrew, or fought back. Paul fought back. He and his mother would battle on deep into the night, driving each other towards madness.

All of us taking acid were fragile beings, some more so than others, and that was why we took the stuff; *because* we could change, because we were not impervious, because we welcomed the precarious tightrope tumble towards (what we knew in faith must be) our truer selves.

I tripped with Paul and his then-girlfriend

once, and it seemed to me that he opened himself
far less to her — showed his true feelings, let go —
than he did with me when we tripped alone. I felt
less jealous after that.

A person's vitality — and I appreciate the
humor of myself, a dead man, speaking of such
things — is difficult to capture in words. Our
friends race through our lives like shooting stars,
and when, of an evening's conversation, we manage to enclose their fire and our own within a few
hours and the space of a room, it is a taste of
eternity, the best of eternity, the true meaning of
friendship.

There are many things I want to say. First is
that Paul's fear fascinated me. I didn't shrink from
it, I *respected* it; I saw it as something noble, something heroic, something I didn't have.

A second thing is that I have come to see LSD
as a metaphor, maybe even a euphemism. At the
time I was taking it, acid was a way of swallowing
and diving into the whole world. If there had been
another way (and surely, if there hadn't been acid,
there would have been another word and symbol
for the same thing), we'd have done that. All we
wanted was total existence.

A third thing is that Paul, whom I'm telling
you about, is no one special. If he hadn't been
Paul so-and-so from Cambridge, Mass., he would
have been somebody else. I could say he was a
mirror of my self during our friendship; but then,
I'm no one, too.

Paul, when we got to know each other and were roaming outer and inner space together — the summer of 1967, a fateful time for psychedelic explorers and other children of the decade — was a young man very obviously on the way up, a teenage publishing whiz riding to the moon on his own guts & energy & imagination & an idea whose time had come (it wasn't till later — November the same year — that *Rolling Stone* came along and started stealing his thunder); however, for what it's worth, he didn't talk much about the magazine and its triumphs while we were together. Occasionally some words about its tribulations, but mostly for openers; quickly we would move to the real meat of our conversations and enthusiasms: politics, the future of our kind, our global community, great ideas, intense consid-erations of how acid really works on the mind (Paul was fascinated for a long time by the transi-tion between ordinary consciousness and tripping, that moment that usually occurs — with the "white lightning" we were taking — sometime in the first half hour or forty minutes after dropping, conceptually a moment but in fact at some point you just find yourself in the *other place*, unmis-takably, and that's what Paul was working on, trying to parse the minutes and seconds to examine as closely as possible that passage to the other place . . . I know he brought calculus, theory of limits, into it somehow, and was very excited by a paragraph in *The Crying of Lot 49* where Thomas Pynchon used the same analogy or analytic device) . . . We talked a lot about political demonstrations, which we attended both as participants and observers, leaving ourselves free in our hearts to tell ourselves we were more one or the other, depending on what was happening — of course I was a reporter, I was there to get the story, if there was one, but there was always more to it than that on some level, and Paul had no professional business at all at these events — we went because it was fun, exciting and important, in one way or another we were involved. We didn't know what was going to happen, and whatever did happen was a part of and reflection of the chemistry of our community, our joint aspirations, our lives. In a way we were like a couple of old boys chasing fires, watching the energy conflagrations, getting off on the event; but we were also firefighters, and we were also the fire itself. I mean we ran, we got our heads hit, we shouted and blocked streets, while we watched. And at home in the loft we talked, about what was happening and would happen, about the ideas and personalities of people like Jerry Rubin and Abbie Hoffman . . . as well as the ditto and especially of course the *actions* of anyone else who stood tall, Rock Scully or Emmett Grogan or Gary Snyder or The Group Image or our friend Linn House. Or LBJ or Bobby Kennedy. There was *so much* going on! We could hardly spend much time discussing the trivialities of publishing a magazine or working for a newspaper.

We were a team, investigating the scene, the seen, the unseen and even what we'd only *imagined* we'd seen. We were a team, but we were also thee and me; and if I talk about your uncertainties, Paul, whatever inner quirks drove you this way and that, it's simply because I have to, because the stories of our lives are the true stories, the only news that can possibly explain or illumine the wondrous events that razzled and dazzled before our eyes in those times — we *were* the events, the sum total of the insides of all those people just like you or like me was the only thing there when you do look closely — that razzled and dazzled before our eyes & ears in those times, and always always will.

VI.

I bought a copy of *Loaded* by the Velvet
Underground when I came out of the woods
for a couple of months in late 1970. I left
Seattle with the album in one arm, sleeping
bag in the other; it was raining half-snowing
and there was very little daylight and the
hitchhiking was poor. The album jacket got
quite wet and I kept it wrapped inside the
sleeping bag after that.

I went to a party Christmas day in
Mendocino and woke up the next morning
with a fever, my first in years. Put me flat
on my back for three days, sweating till my
bag was soaked, struggling up occasionally
to put more wood in the stove. In a geo-
desic dome.

A week or so later I first found myself
in a place that had electricity . . . well anyway the building where people ate and
cooked and hung out had electricity, and a
phonograph, and I played my record just as
many times as I could get away with.

Quietly, not wanting to attract too
much attention in a room that was always
filled with people, many of them strangers,
I listened to "Cool It Down" and "New Age"
and flipped into paroxysms of ecstasy.

"I'll come running to you, honey when
you want me . . . "

(Feel the musical and emotional pressure build up, singing through my blood-
stream; feel my brain bursting with the joy
of each additional note)

"Something's got a hold on me, and I
don't know what . . . "

(Now a moment of release, stately
march music, transcendent, glorious, full of
energy and dignity)

"It's the beginning of a new age . . . "

Later in the day I'd be sawing wood,
break through the log, and hear that
music. It was a sunny January. I traveled
from woman to woman, and my heart was
light.

"Hey baby if you want it so fast, don't
you know honey that it ain't gonna last? Of

　　　　　　　　　　　　Paul Williams

course, you know it makes no difference to me.

"You'd better cool it down . . . "

I was free at that moment. I was free as a bird is free who doesn't see how high he's flown. In February I took acid and dived into a mountain stream fresh out of the ice fields, six thousand feet up, in Siskiyou County. Nothing could bring me down. I was suffering from seven different kinds of grief and confusion, but it didn't matter; I dried myself off and kept heading back north (in Mendocino my standing joke was that I'd come south for the winter) (like if someone from Labrador said that to you on a cold, rainy day in New York).

Loaded (a classic album, one of the greats, search for it, cherish it) was the music of that moment. Back in the woods we didn't have no recorded music — which only partly explains why *Loaded* is the only record I can remember getting into that year. The Velvet Underground's music, starting with "Sister Ray" on their second album and continuing through the entire third and fourth albums, is like a map of my mind, '68 – '71, and believe me that was tough territory for cartographers. Lou Reed struck a chord of sheer genius, and pounded it till both he and I, singer and listener, fell down in exhaustion.

Those were the days, my friend.

Funny that I should talk like this, because the paradise days for me were the days of the *third* Velvet album, the one with "Pale Blue Eyes" and "Candy Says" and "Jesus." Lou Reed singing like an absolute saint, like the Jack of Hearts. Paradise days in Mendocino (spring '69, happiness of unintentional community, Raven born, good weather, good friends, bountiful weed and abalone) we played that record night and day till we wore it flat.

Loaded is after, after I moved to Canada in search of surer paradise, after the third Velvet album failed to sell despite its unearthly beauty, and so they made *Loaded*, a rock 'n' roll album full of likely hit singles, as a last try . . . (Lou cracked up before the LP came out, and vanished back to Long Island.) Some of the finest hard rock music ever recorded is on that album, culminating in "Oh Sweet Nothing," a note of sweet sad loving triumph and fullness-in-emptiness that will ring throughout the universe forever.

And by the time I went south for my winter vacation I'd already been up to my ears in trouble and only eternal dumb optimism could have kept me believing and trying with such startling intensity. I made love to five women during my swing south, and fell in love with three of them. Delicious madness.

After paradise, the struggles to regain it; then luxurious freedom when you first let go for a moment. Vacation.

And then the terror, the bottomless loneliness and uncertainty, when you find you just can't get a grip again . . .

VII.

I know better than most people that our lives
never end; but the truth is they also end at every
moment. The last few months of my life I became
quite obsessed with mirrors — I mean getting
stoned and staring into my own eyes in a mirror,
seeing that creature watching me, staring at it, at
him, falling ever deeper into terror and awareness
and awe. There was something very sinister about
doing this; I tried to stop, but there was something very seductive in it too, just one more drug I
finally found no reason to resist.

I now believe our lives end every time we see
our own reflections.

Paul and I sat on opposite ends of my bed,
staring at my Felix-The-Cat clock (with pendulum
tail) on the far wall, and laughing. The first sensu-

ous, funny, mind-lightening sensations of oncoming rush were hitting us, revealing in the space of seconds 1001 great jokes about the universe, jokes we each perceived independently but laughed at together. Our thoughts stretched like rubber faces in amusement hall mirrors, and though we saw the hands of the clock clearly, we had trouble getting them to "mean" anything.

"When did we drop?"

"About 12:30."

"So it's only — what? Twenty minutes? Impossible . . . "

(laughter)

Then beautiful things would start happening with, oh, the cracks in the ceiling. And the air would start to shimmer like waves of the ocean, and I would just let go and let it wash over and through me.

Paul was struggling with something. I didn't interfere; it didn't seem to be time yet. His face looked ecstatically happy, with just a slight shadow of worry starting somewhere low and getting a bit larger every moment. I looked away; my own face must have been a picture of changing emotions, but then it passed and I felt serene again. Really so lucky to be alive at this moment. I gave him an inquisitive look, with a smile; he smiled back, and we both started grinning like idiots.

"Twenty minutes? But . . . "

" . . . s-strong . . . "

Then I had to lie down again. I could hear him breathing heavily, trying to contain the rush.

The story begins in Harvard Square. A light green Volkswagen is driving into the Square, on Concord Avenue, Cambridge, fortyish man in the driver's seat, teenage boy beside him.

The man says something, and suddenly the teenager opens the door on his side and turns to get out. The car slows down but doesn't stop. The boy says something to the driver, and jumps. The impact of his feet hitting the pavement is not enough to hurt him or knock him down, but it's a shock; he feels it all through his body. A moment ago he felt suspended in dreadful motion, the walls of Their prison already closing in. Now to his astonishment that motion is reversed; he lets the impact shudder through him, then walks off into his own universe not listening to the words of the adult shouting after him.

Paul was seventeen; the adult was not his father but his girlfriend's father; what he'd said was, "I think you should let me take you to Mass. Mental Health for observation." Paul had called the girl after a climactic fight with his mother; he'd been hiding in a cemetery, certain that his mother had sent the police out looking for him. He said he needed help, and Sara let him come over, though their year-long romance had come to a bitter end ten days earlier.

At her house they played the new Beatles record ("When I was younger, so much younger than today / I never needed anybody's help in any way"), but though she understood it was a message from him to her there was nothing she could do, and she had to tell him so again.

Her father knew only that she had been under tremendous pressure to have sex with this boy, pressure she hadn't given in to but which had caused her enormous anxiety. He, the father, thought this a sick, deranged thing for anyone to do to a sixteen-year-old girl; he could see how tense Sara became after Paul called that day; and he resolved, after an unsatisfying phone conversation with the boy's mother, that he personally would try to see that this boy got psychiatric help.

Sara asked Paul to leave, and her father offered, rather insistently, to drive him to Harvard Square. As they got near the Square, he told Paul he was taking him to MMH for testing. (Paul knew this guy had called his mother and damned him as a sex fiend.) Paul jumped from the car, feeling hatred, relishing the melodrama as some kind of partial antidote to the pain of Sara's rejection.

. . . After I walked out of that guy's car in Harvard Square, I truly had nowhere to go. I was between two women: one who wouldn't take me, one who wouldn't leave me alone. I did go back to my mother's house for a few days, but the pressure was

unrelieved, the situation unresolvable.
There really is no solution for parent/ado-
lescent conflicts except letting the break
take place. Some stormy August night of
her fury and mine, I walked out of the
house and the argument (Mom screaming
after me ordering me to return), walked to
Route 2 less than a mile away along so-
familiar streets & thumbed down a pickup
truck which got me as far as Lexington. It
took me twenty-four hours to get to New
York City.

Somewhere along the Mass. Pike two
guys picked me up, your usual unknowable
night drivers with basically good inten-
tions. I was completely inexperienced, at
hitchhiking, at life; their car broke down,
& since they were going to NY I waited with
them at the service station until they
learned for sure that they'd have to wait till
morning, & then since I didn't know any
better and was reluctant to go out on the
road again at four a.m. and actually believed that a ride to New York was something rare & valuable, I agreed to wait the
night. They got a motel room with two
beds, I slept alone in one bed after they
wouldn't let me sleep on the floor and I
refused to share a bed, they slept in the
other together not their usual arrangement
I believe, and in the morning with the car

still not ready to roll at eleven I hit the road
again.

Earlier, much earlier that forty-eight-
hour day, I had gone into Harvard Square by
bus and visited with Martha, a girl I hadn't
seen for several months, a girl I'd had a
terrific, very sexual (unrequited) crush on
in the winter and early spring when we
acted together in a production of *Gigi* (I was
Gaston LaChaille, man-of-the-world, what a
joke). Martha was short, sultry, tough and
energetic, curly black hair & great small
figure, she hung out with older men and
dressed in dark colors to set off her bright
face, and radiated a contradictory, delicious
aura of class and availability. She was obviously dangerous — as my friends pointed
out to me. But I fell like a ton of bricks, as
soon as I found myself in the incredible
position of having momentarily caught her
attention, and despite my already confused
involvement with and deep affection for
(count them) two of her classmates. I rel-
ished the confusion, felt flattered and excited, felt love.

Which never came to much, she had
another boyfriend, I tried hard (one of *his*
friends threatened me with a gun at a party)
and won some respect but no solace. I felt
pain, and started writing blues songs.
Months went by; I stopped trying. And then

almost by chance I dropped by her apartment building while wandering around Cambridge that August day and found her home, alone.

I told her about me and Sara, how she'd come back from England a month earlier and the whole awful story of how our initial joy at being reunited turned into terrible distance & mutual agony & bitterness & break-up. We talked about each other too, uncovered and cleared up some misunderstandings I never knew existed, and it all set me free, my pain and sincerity about Sara so evident and Martha opened to me as never before, cradled me in her arms and I couldn't hold back, I tried to make love to her, tugging at her low-cut black jersey and rolling around on the floor with her while she fought me off, laughing, affectionate, but firm.

So I didn't get what I wanted but I felt good anyway, felt very good and then forgot about it in the fight with my mother and flight to the highway. And then as I lay on that silly motel bed with my white sweater (which I'd taken off to use as a pillow when I thought I was going to be on the floor), I made the wonderful discovery that my sweater was full of her scent, some perfume plus natural body-musk or whatever, and I lay there ecstatic just breathing in the smell of her and remembering the warmth of her presence those many hours earlier. It was satori, totally unexpected reaffirmation, that scent magically cutting through all my road loneliness and sense of being lost in the universe and rekindling the promise of paradise.

Martha Martha Martha, I knew even then I'd never see you again, but my message is: thanks for everything. Whatever desire is, I still feel it when I think of you.

And finally (because we have to telescope everything in these life-stories) the other image of that trip to New York is standing in a Manhattan police station — I called Mom some time after arriving at my friends' place in Brooklyn, made the mistake of telling her where I was so she wouldn't worry, she threatened to send the police there and I promised to come back to keep her from doing so, explained I had no money and she said I had only to turn myself in to the cops, as there was a multistate alert out looking for me (all bullshit, I now realize), and they'd get me home — trying to turn myself in (Manhattan so as to minimize chances of involving my friends in Brooklyn, science fiction fans, the whole thing just embarrassed me hugely and I didn't want them to be hassled or even to know), and having the cops say

they weren't interested, and sitting there
adrift just watching them bring in prosti-
tutes, and hearing (this is the key detail)
Bob Dylan's big hit "Like A Rolling Stone"
wailing from some desk sergeant's portable
radio.

The thing about looking in mirrors is that it
reveals the depth of our situation. I mean literally.
What we see, most of the time when we look at
the world, is surfaces. Looking into my own eyes
in a mirror reflection, I found it difficult to stay on
the surface. I kept seeing through, through to the
consciousness behind the eyes, truly the most
terrifying sight those eyes ever looked on.
Looking in a mirror is looking back. In our
little lives we are constantly looking forward,
striving at all costs to avoid remembering that we
are treading on the surface of the infinite. The
name of our fear is acrophobia; we are afraid to
look down, afraid of falling into forever.
You suppose I can speak calmly of these
things now; I am dead, I have no body, I have
nowhere to fall and nothing to fall with. You are
wrong, for reasons I cannot even begin to sug-
gest. I can only say that, since I escaped from life,
I have been more alive and more afraid of falling
than I ever was before.
Don Juan says that fear is the first enemy of a
man of knowledge. So fear is inevitably part of the
story of such a person's life, the struggle with fear,

we embrace that struggle if we wish to have any
story at all.

The second enemy is clarity, & that's what I
expired of.

Paul was frightened by his own madness. He
felt he couldn't control it; he worried about what
he might say or do when the drug took over. Acid
would make him panicky about physical things: he
thought he couldn't breathe, he thought his heart
would snap if he didn't do something about the
anxiety he was feeling. There was for him on a trip
this drastic sense of the absolute importance of
every moment. Not so much cosmic consciousness as a sense that the building was going to
burn down in the next thirty seconds.

He was not one of those trippers who sit
almost motionless for thirteen hours. Sometimes I
felt that his spine was a tuning fork, and that I
could see the restless energy vibrating off his body
in waves into the air. But it wasn't the mindless
restlessness of the amphetamine heads from East
7th Street — I romanticized Paul as a doer, an
achiever, a worthy companion for the dynamic &
independent journalist and novelist I imagined
myself to be in daydreams.

What he saw in me I still don't know, I'm not
certain, but it must have been something because
he kept coming 'round, almost every day for a
while there. And always, whatever else was happening in our crazy lives, things were relaxed and

open between us.

It was a great relief to enjoy such friendship.

Paul and Sara met at a Buckingham party in May, 1964. Buckingham was a girls' school in Cambridge which collaborated with Browne & Nichols — the boys' school that Paul attended — in certain areas, notably dramatics. Paul's main contact with the opposite sex in those high school days was during and as a result of dramatic presentations. He stage-managed a coeducational production of *Patience* at B&N in the fall of '63, then acted at Buckingham in the early spring in *The Grass Harp*. It was someone he knew through the latter experience who ran into him in Harvard Square that Saturday, a "complex" day he said which means a lot of different things were happening to him and so he was full of loose energy and relatively outgoing & unselfconscious, and invited him to this nearby afternoon party which apparently had a shortage of males.

With the result that he met Sara and started joking with her about something silly and the conversation went on and on and got interesting and intense for both of them and much later (after dashing out of the party to keep an appointment with his science fiction friends in Harvard Square & then dashing back) he walked her home and made a tentative date to see her the following weekend.

And walked from her house near Concord

Avenue in seventh heaven, in love no less and for
the first time, it was late at night and as he walked
by the old school where he spent the fifth & sixth
grades, hallowed ground, turned in the gate and
romped through the playground, alone in the
moonlight with his memories and his joy, realizing
that for all these years (five) his ideal lover had
been a girl from sixth grade whom he'd seen
exactly once since graduation & took her to a
museum & couldn't talk — a smart blonde eva-
nescent dream — replaced at last by sassy and
sweet flesh-and-blood brunette Sara, promise of a
universe of wonders, the beginning of a new age.

                                    Paul Williams

VIII.

In the fall of 1965 Paul left Cambridge to go to
college near Philadelphia. He had decided on this
particular college, Swarthmore, because it had a
good reputation, it was small, it was coeducational, and it was near a big city but not in one.
In his heart I think he dreamed of the magical
environment of the tiny, male & female, intellectually stimulating classroom of his elementary school
days. Good friendships & fine adventures & satisfying work. He had discovered himself in that
classroom. Swarthmore seemed — from the college catalogues and his brief visit there — like it
could be the same kind of place.

But there are no repetitions in our lives. Paul
at seventeen was not the same person he'd been
at nine — or he was the same person, but at a

different point in his trajectory. Nothing could be like it was. Paul entered Swarthmore in September full of tormented love for Sara and very uncertain of his own identity after a summer of ever-heightening conflicts with his mother . . . conflicts too large to be easily assimilable into any kind of solid world-concept. He didn't know what was going on. But he did know he needed something he wasn't getting.

It wasn't the sort of thing you could speak to an advisor about. What he needed was the feeling of holding and being held.

And he did the only thing that any of us can do at any age when we feel that need: crawled on his hands and knees, into the darkness.

Darkness. At the moment that I died, gulping my last at the bottom of that foolish pond, my spirit jumped blindly into darkness, that same darkness that has marked the road ahead of me since I was in the womb, the only way out of here, the unlit area, what hasn't been seen yet.

I drowned in the summer of '68, roughly at midpoint in the chronology of this story I'm trying to tell you. There are reasons and reasons why I'm writing this book, but one of them's just simply to say that death's not the end of the story.

Sara returned from her six months in England in mid-July. Immediately, she and Paul resumed their courtship; immediately, both of them knew

     Paul Williams

or should've known that what had been before was gone forever and that what was now was impossibly fragile, requiring far more care and tenderness, understanding, than they in their mutual inexperience were capable of.

But of course they had to try. And when Paul entered Swarthmore in the fall he was still trying — for months he sent her angry, begging letters — though he knew it was way past time to stop.

Intellectually, college was a disappointment. He was surprised at the limited nature of the courses available to freshmen, and even more surprised, when he started going to the classes he'd selected for his first semester, how little he cared about any of them. He couldn't read his survey-of-Western-history text. He couldn't write the papers and exams for his introduction-to-philosophy class. He couldn't even go to his Russian class, after the first month or so. And it hurt him to discover that his beloved extracurriculars, dramatics, the school newspaper, had also lost all their relevance to his life somewhere in the gulf between his last autumn of high school and his first autumn at college.

He got a gig at the college radio station, playing rock and roll records in the morning and blues at night. That absorbed him, excited him, gave him pleasure. (He used to take the train into Philly to look for interesting records at a place on 13th Street that sold dj copies of singles at 10¢ apiece.)

And he enjoyed hanging out, in the dorm, at the snack bar, with his friends, other kids like himself who had the credentials and the raw ability but just couldn't get into the grind of college life. The bohemian faction.

But the music and the hanging out weren't enough to offset the three dominant adjectives of Paul's life at Swarthmore: bored, lonely, and restless.

He started hitchhiking a lot, to New York and Boston, searching for something, anything, that would bring him back to life.

I hitchhiked between Boston and Philadelphia so many times in '65 and '66 that I wore a groove in the earth. Not so many times the full route, but rather a predominance of NY – Phila. runs while I was still in Swarthmore, and then mainly NY – Boston after I dropped out and returned to Cambridge. New York was new to me, a place I'd visited a few times in childhood and then passed through — experiencing the place intensely, but still in transit — occasionally during pre-college adolescence. And now discovering, still in tiny doses, a fragment of the city's geography each time, but what doses! What fragments! Sleeping in Van Cortland Park, running wild with wild new-found friends on the winter beach at night at Coney Island. New York people, the ones

I met, were crazier and freer; because of the
all-night subways, and whatever, so many
young people in a world of their own, it was
a place where you didn't have to go back to
your dorm or your mother.

And it was a place where you could do
things. It was in New York that I started my
magazine.

I was bored, y'know, like the man says,
bored and restless and lonely, I couldn't do
the schoolwork or get it on with the
Swarthmore scene and it made me feel very
insecure, I'd built myself up from terrible
inversion with people in seventh grade to a
certain self-confidence & resultant fluidity
based completely on my output, the high
school extracurriculars and the science
fiction magazine I published on the side
and so forth, the stuff I was doing made me
feel sure of myself which in turn made it
possible for me to run with, have fun with,
other people. Which reached a peak in the
fall of my senior year, I was accomplishing
things left and right, I had the respect of
the young women I worked with in the
dramatics club and then even the attention
of a few of them, I was writing a lot and I
even tried briefly to study the guitar, a
whirlwind of energy and though still shy
inside I hardly had time to notice — and
then there I was in college, at Swarthmore,

unable to open a book or even write a story
for the newspaper, hanging out, doing nothing . . . Doing nothing! A total disaster for
one whose ability to function in the world
was based solely on his pride in the things
he was doing, I needed desperately many
things including that holding and being
held but most of all I needed something to
do, my inability to *do anything* at college
was bringing me face to face with the most
horrible self-doubt I have ever experienced.

So finally when the idea came or came
back to start a magazine about this rock
music I was so in love with, arriving in my
head complete with a plan as to just exactly
how I could do it and what to do first and
what would happen, it was a godsend — a
tremendous gift of energy — my salvation.

And it married me to New York —
though I didn't consummate the marriage
and move there till much later, eleven
months later, December of 1966 — because
that was where the rock music business was
on the East Coast, that was the place I
needed to go simply to do the very first
thing, which was obtain some new records
so I could review them.

I conceived of the magazine as a weekly,
believe it or not, which would review new
albums but especially singles, intelligently
rather than with the usual hype, as a serv-

ice both to music lovers and the music business. I knew about the trade magazines, had been into them since I started listening to rock a year earlier (and even in the sixth grade I'd been addicted to top-40 lists, actually bicycling into Belmont Center the hour that I knew the sheets would arrive in the local record store because I couldn't wait to see what the positions would be this week, I was a pest, a fanatic), but I felt the trade magazines were inadequate because — just like the "fan" magazines from the opposite side — they *didn't take the music seriously*. I knew that the earnestness which my friends and I felt wasn't being expressed in print.

And something else — it wasn't just love for the music — I wanted to start a magazine. And I'd read in a "fanzine," an amateur publication from the science fiction underworld, an article by James Warren, publisher of *Famous Monsters of Filmland* and *Help!*, in which he talked about how to start a magazine; he said that what you need most of all is a subject that a lot of people are into that nobody is doing a magazine about. I read that & believed it & even mentioned to some people in Cambridge in the summer of '65 before I went to Swarthmore, when a folk music paper called *Broadside* was the best-read publication in town, that somebody ought to start a magazine about rock 'n' roll. I couldn't do it 'cause I was about to go off to college and get involved in that, but whoever did pick up the idea would meet with certain success.

And I forgot, and then got ever deeper into rock via the college radio station, and then was standing in the town of Swarthmore, a tiny commercial district beyond the great lawn of the college, standing in a drugstore reading a story about the Yardbirds in a fan magazine and when I read that both they *and* the Rolling Stones had got their start in a club in Richmond, England called the Crawdaddy Club it just hit me out of nowhere that that would be the name of my magazine and then it hit me that I was really going to publish the magazine and I could do the first issue in New York during the four-day intersession after exams and mimeo it at Ted's house and then . . . I paid for the fan mag and walked back across the tracks to the campus very excited and completely lost in a truly enormous daydream.

Paul, I never told you then, but I knew what you were afraid of. You were afraid of falling — from your precarious success, your sanity, your self-confidence, your ability to keep it all together

week after week. You were not unaware of the
brittle side of your New York reality.

You were right. Hey, you must have been
scared when I fell off the planet! That was some
leap you took: New York City to California, owner
of a monthly magazine to stoker of a wood fire in
an airtight heater in a cabin in a redwood forest.
Did I really make you jump like that?

No, I don't kid myself. I saw the whole fight.
I know my death was just the final blow. I was
your trainer, remember? Remember that STP trip
where you went three rounds with Otis Driftwood
before driving him from the house — that cavern-
ous loft, last loft, on Broome Street — and collaps-
ing in my arms? I brought you back by dabbing at
your face with a wet towel. It was a stormy summer night, you had your shirt off and the image of
you as a wounded prizefighter just hit me in a
satori flash. There was nothing to say. I massaged
your shoulder muscles, trying to ease your spirit
and let you know everything was all right. Every
now and then I would break out laughing — big
grin turning to sound — remembering the look on
Otis's face.

The boxing metaphor. Why do fighters fight,
anyway? Why do any of us do what we do? Once I
found out the answer, I could leave with a satisfied
mind.

I don't mean to say I made a conscious
decision to leave. New York, yes, I planned to
leave New York, Paul and I were going to drive to

Alaska, stopping on the way to attend the Demo-
cratic Convention in Chicago (I learned recently
that my credentials arrived at the *Voice* two days
after my death), we'd both had enough of the city
& the work we were doing and Paul's life with
Trina had blown up in his face, but I never intended to quit this valley altogether, we were
heading for new and better earthly adventures,
that's all.

But life itself explodes in our faces sometimes.
It was just one of those things — call it poor judg-
ment, an accident, a willful confrontation with
Fate, it doesn't matter to me what you call it — I
was alone at the country house, I guess I was
pretty stoned, I felt like going swimming (I was
very impressed once on a trip at Roots when you
suddenly took off all your clothes and jumped into
that same pond and swam around in the evening
light for what must have been fifteen minutes),
and then when I was out there, the water was so
beautiful at first, completely relaxing, but I got this
pain in my side . . .

Paul, I don't know if I'm writing this book *to*
you or about you. And I guess you don't know
sometimes if you're writing the book or I am. I call
it a collaboration. What you choose to believe
depends on your definition of reality, I guess.

When I jumped into the darkness, I was a
mouse, not even a rat, deserting the sinking ship
of my body. I didn't want to do it but finally I had
no choice, I couldn't raise that thing, I just lost

control somehow. I felt like Alice falling down the rabbit-hole, tumbling in a spiral, into the infinite. I didn't know if I would ever hit bottom.

I still don't know.

Death is as strange an experience as I ever could have imagined. I don't know if I'm here, or not here. I know I don't have any body, and I feel I don't have a mind, either — I don't know what I have — but I know I have something. I can feel, I can perceive. Yesterday I rode across the Manhattan Bridge at sunset, on the D train, that deep orange western light silhouetting the half-lit frames of Wall Street skyscrapers that weren't yet built when I went under. I'm aware, I can move around; I can even talk about it.

I can talk about it through your pen, your mind, nothing that can be distinguished from you in the perception of the living. And I have access — in varying degrees — to other vehicles as well. I hope what I'm saying doesn't make you feel uncomfortable. I don't believe you're any less you by being part me. But this conversation is a little like looking in the mirrors — sometimes it's better not to go too deep into things.

I want to talk about you, not me. I like your substantiality. When you're dead, you'll know how I feel.

In 1964, before he met Sara, Paul applied for and got a scholarship to a summer program that involved four weeks of Russian study at Choate

Academy, followed by a five-week visit to the
Soviet Union, with the result that Paul and Sara
had a little less than two months together before
Paul had to go to Connecticut. But what months:
rich in affection and discovery, little games and
private jokes, approach, first love like brother-and-
sister intimacy as imagined by an only child
(which Sara was; Paul had two younger brothers),
meeting on the banks of the Charles, Boston side
of the Lars Andersen Bridge, lying on the grass
and flirting, employing their mutual huge intelligence to explore marvelous realms of verbal
silliness, for the fun and privacy of it & as a way to
express deep feelings.

And when he went to Choate (he was just
sixteen; she would be fifteen in August) they
exchanged letters, long playful earnest letters,
every day for a month; and then, with less fre-
quency due to technical difficulties, more letters,
to and from Kiev, Moscow, Samarkand, Transcau-
casia and Alma Ata. In village squares halfway
around the world, Paul chattered excitedly in
broken Russian, but still longed as only a sixteen-
year-old can long for Sara's arms around him in his
hotel room late at night.

So, back in Cambridge at the end of the
summer after a final visit to Poland — Auschwitz
and Chopin and a drunken night with college
students near the remains of the Warsaw Ghetto
— Paul was ready for the next stage of his teenage
love affair.

Sara was not as ready, reluctant to let him put his arms around her, not eager for the trouble she knew would follow. She held him off with words, words given power by the ever-deepening affection they expressed. And he in turn was distracted by all the busy-ness of autumn, the whirlwind activity (from *My Fair Lady* to college applications to *Moby Dick*) of his senior year in high school, first semester, climax of a long career.

They saw each other when they could, and it wasn't until the cast parties for *My Fair Lady* that things began to unravel.

I'll interrupt Don for a moment here. He's said a little about who he thinks he is, as well as quite a bit about who he thinks I am; now maybe I should say something about who *I* think he is, or rather, who I think is writing this book.

Naturally, I mostly feel that I'm writing it; I can feel my body sitting on this chair, I hear my thought and see my fingers hit the typewriter keys and watch the words appear on the blank page in front of me. I think of "Don" as something more than a premise, there is a consciousness there that I can't wholly account for, but still something less than a "real," living person.

But in order to write Don's segments, I first have to in some sense conjure up Don himself, from my memory (prodded by grass and sometimes a glance through his book). And isn't that at least one of the places where dead people live — in the memories of their friends? Maybe "the spirit world" is just another name for the collective unconscious.

But Don says he lives through me and others in a more active sense, not the deep-freeze image I get when I think of something living in memory. And I have to believe him, because the origin of anything I write that's "good" is mysterious to me, it's like asking where the music comes from. The writer may offer a more articulate answer, but he is as ignorant as all other creators of where the inspiration originates. I don't doubt the Creator Herself is ignorant, working in the dark — on Her own lofty level, of course.

But I'm too full of ideas. That's why I'm happy to have Don tell the story — he seems to focus more on the feelings. And what I *feel*, you see — far beyond anything I might think — is that Don McNeill is indeed here and actively collaborating on this book; and I'm enjoying his presence very much.

Thanks, Paul. I'm going to give you a chapter, so I want to be sure to get the last word in this one.

IX.

Relationships with women/relationships
with men. I have more (and less) to say on
the subject every day. Definitely not the
sort of inquiry one can exhaust in a lifetime. Where do we go from here?

I first met Judy in the spring of 1964,
less than a month after I met Sara. It was
the afternoon of the last day of school (junior year). I had to return a manuscript to
the yearbook photographer, and I knew
where I could find him: at the Simon house,
central watering hole for the Cambridge
chic segment of our class, which I guess
included everyone whose parents didn't
expect him or her home at any particular
hour. It was a place to hang out, opulent

Brattle Street house with Picassos on the
wall, Toulouse-Lautrec in the bathroom,
mommy dead of her own hand and daddy
never around. Scene of frequent large parties and neverending small ones. I had
been there only once before, a large party,
during which I got turned on to Bo Diddley,
"I'm A Man."

I walked around the empty house, left
the manuscript on the kitchen table, put the
record I'd just bought (*Just Dave Van Ronk*)
on the stereo and got into a brief, friendly
conversation with a girl I didn't know who'd
wandered in from the backyard pool in her
bathing suit. She was short, with curly
brown hair, and her small breasts were
almost completely visible inside the loose-
fitting suit. I found her incredibly attractive. The next day I visited the house again,
and we went swimming together.

I was enticed, but hardly bold. She
turned out to be a friend of Sara's. I went to
Russia, and we met again in the fall when
Judy got a small part in the musical I was
stage-managing. I was very busy during all
rehearsals, and we didn't talk much (and I
was always with Sara on the weekends), but
I was conscious of Judy's presence. In an
abstract way — since after all, what could I
do about it? — I wanted her.

And then, at one of the series of cast

parties that followed completion of the
musical, we zeroed in on each other,
danced cheek to cheek and body to body
(to the singing of Françoise Hardy, LPs that
Sara's father brought back from Europe,
the essential slow music for every party as
the Stones and the Kingsmen were the
essential rockers), and it was too fine to
forget, we couldn't ignore our mutual
attraction after that.

Sara couldn't ignore it either (though
she tried for a while); she didn't go to most
of those parties, but of course she had
friends who did.

It's easier for me to let Don tell this
story than to try and tell it myself. I feel a
need to justify myself, to protect friends
and to remember details accurately, all
things that get in the way of just telling a
straightforward story. When Don writes
about my past, even though he uses my
fingers, I feel less self-conscious; all my
effort goes to letting him come through
loud and clear. I don't have to think about
what he's saying about me.

I don't have to think. And I'm starting
to realize that, even when I write in the first
person, as here, I'm not the author of this
book; I'm just a character who gets to de-
liver soliloquies now and then — under the

playwright's direction, of course.

So am I writing this chapter on my own, or aren't I? I throw the question into the air, and the answer comes back: "You can call it whatever you like, as long as you don't stop writing."

Yes, sir.

Relationships with men. Bill Richards had been my friend — one of my only friends — since early in the eighth grade, his first year at Browne & Nichols. We became friends on the soccer field as much as anywhere else, talking and hacking around on the sidelines whenever someone wasn't forcing us to play. I liked his sense of humor. He would get onto a word — like "fern," which he got from the Steve Allen show, or "sexy" — and use it in every sentence.

We had a lot in common, lots to share and talk about. We were down on athletics and school spirit in general. We both liked reading strange magazines — *Help!*, *Monocle* — and science fiction. We went to dusty second-hand bookstores together. And we were both Democrats in a school dominated by Republicans — I remember running over to the other side of Harvard Square, near Bill's house, one schoolday when we should have been somewhere else, to see

President-elect Kennedy come out of Arthur
Schlesinger's house. Schlesinger's son was
in the class behind us at school — like Bill,
like Sara the child of a Harvard professor —
like me, too, except that my father had been
an MIT professor, and now he was in Montreal with his second wife.

Bill and I continued to find interests in
common, year after year. We read *Lolita*
simultaneously, covertly, in the ninth grade.
We passed notes through five years of
French classes, and three years of Russian.
We wrote and mimeographed a rebellious
pamphlet, which the slick headmaster of
the school talked us out of distributing. We
went to the Boston Arts Festival to see Pete
Seeger and *Man and Superman*. We listened
to Bob Dylan together, then later the Rolling
Stones. And we fell in love with the same
woman.

Judy, of course.

A woman can change a man's life without becoming his constant companion. Judy
and I were never together for long. Eventually, in Mendocino, 1969, we did spend
some time in the same house — even in the
same bed, briefly — but I think we were
further apart in those months than at any
other time in our lives.

But in 1964, when I was sixteen and in

love with Sara, seeing her on the weekends
and hanging out with Bill Richards on week-
days, Judy's very occasional proximity to
me was enough to overthrow the whole
rational course of my relationships with
women and men.

What happened is . . . well, I don't know
what happened. For the longest time I was
just another lonely teenager; and then Sara
came into my life, a real beauty and a soul-
companion, and you'd think, after my years
as an ugly duckling, I'd be humble enough
to stay satisfied.

But I have a tendency in my life to slide
from humility to arrogance with surprising
ease. I mean, since Sara liked me, it wasn't
so difficult for me to imagine that other
women might also find me attractive. I was
aware of Judy, and pleased that she got a
choral part in *My Fair Lady*. And she, for
whatever reason, maybe just ordinary
female rivalry (she and Sara were school-
mates), seemed to be aware of me.

Sara was a friend, someone I could talk
to; our love was based heavily on our ability to communicate, sensitivity, giving each
other comfort by sharing little awarenesses
about the world. We were close enough to
be able to poke fun at each other, which is
real intimacy, sitting on the grass at night
by the river, me with my head in her lap,

making up stories about the mysterious box
that made clicking noises behind us.

Judy was different, there was a feeling
of intensity I'd get from her, talking with
her or looking at her from a distance, less
comforting than being with Sara, but more
exciting. Sometimes. Other times she just
made me nervous. I didn't know what was
going on in her head. But we'd talk backstage for a few minutes now and then, and
once I got invited over to her house and I
thought Sara was going to come and she
didn't, wasn't invited, and oh-so-hesitantly
(and with some shock, amazement, not
really arrogant or self-confident yet) I began
to figure out what was happening. I was
excited, nervous, I wanted to confide in
(brag to) somebody, and of course the only
possible person was Bill.

And that round of parties began, J. &
me dancing dreamy-eyed, and I began to
feel more and more desire for Judy, not that
I loved Sara less but the situation was getting complicated . . .

Two things happened: Sara finally
confronted me about Judy (in my naïveté,
I really didn't think she knew), and Bill and
I and Sara and Judy all attended the same
party. It was New Year's Eve.

Sara had informed me several weekends earlier that she wasn't going to be in

school next term (February – June). Her parents were going to England for six months, and she was going with them. Given the situation I was in, I guess I accepted this news with a mixture of regret and relief. It was like my trip to Russia, only longer — of course we'd write to each other, and we'd still be the same people, in love with each other, when she returned.

I still didn't tell her about Judy — what can you say, anyway? That you *think* this other girl is making a pass at you, and if so, you don't think you can resist her? Better, in this situation at least, to wait and pray for good timing.

But she knew, and she sprang it on me, in a roundabout, playful way, finding "significance" in an oblique comment I'd made to Bill in a marginal note in William Golding's *Free Fall*, a novel we were reading for English class. She put me on the spot, and in the course of the difficult conversation that followed we opened up to each other more than we had in a long time. Her anger turned to understanding as my evasiveness turned to embarrassed confession; and soon we found ourselves closer to each other and more in love than ever, which was perhaps something more than either of us had hoped for . . .

This was only a day or two before New

Year's Eve, and so we went to the party full
of warmth for each other and with little
attention to spare for anyone else. Sara's
father drove us over there, and we stopped
and picked up Bill on the way — he hadn't
felt like going, and I kind of urged him to,
maybe because I was getting pretty cocky
and I wanted him to see Judy, the girl I'd
been telling him about, wanted him to see
how pretty she was and thus appreciate my
awe at my own good fortune.

The joke was on me. Bill complimented
me on my good taste in friends, all right. So
did Judy. They hit it off right away.

Wallowing in my own past, now ten
years gone or more, I wonder if I've learned
anything. And, just to take myself off the
hook for a moment, if any of us ever learn
anything or if, where the heart is concerned, it's even a question of learning . . .
Maybe the heart is a constant, constant K,
beating away unalterably while the equa-
tions shift around it. Lust has a greater
value one year, dignity another, then still
another year lust *is* dignity and time is the
only variable, will we ever find a moment
alone or . . . ? The heart meanwhile doesn't
care, it just feels what's there to be felt, if
anything, sleeping and waking at odd
hours . . .

My heart woke up in the winter of 1965
expecting a great dose of romantic love —
which never arrived, so I settled for a
double-shot of romantic pain and loneliness, terrible stuff but easy to get off on.
Besides, it's always available.

After that New Year's Eve party Bill
started taking Judy to the movies, walking
her home, long talks on the doorstep outside her apartment, that sort of thing. Sara
didn't leave for England till late in January.
I didn't exactly ignore Judy during those
weeks; but I didn't give her my full attention, either. I was in a dilemma: I naturally
wanted to be with Sara because she was the
girl I loved and she was going away. But I
wanted to be with Judy, too, because she
was the love coming towards me, anticipa-
tion, my future.

And I could in fact feel love for both
women (is a fifteen-year-old girl a woman?
Yes, of course she is. That is one of the
Mysteries I have somehow always intui-
tively understood).

I would have been better off had I believed (and felt) that there's only one Miss
or Mister Right in this world for each of us.
Intellectually, I was not unwilling to embrace this dictum. But circumstances con-
spired to make me feel more than I might
have thought possible; and there was that

in me that wouldn't let me deny my feelings. So I couldn't reject either of these
people — or Bill, who was also a factor now.
But neither could I tell either one that she
was the only person in the world for me,
which no doubt is what we all want to hear.

I just wandered on in my own unde-
fined direction, waiting to see what would
happen.

And Sara went to England — which
didn't altogether take her out of the picture,
since right away we started exchanging love
letters, stirring up new and complex emotions — and Judy and Bill got closer and
became "a couple," without Judy and me
really renouncing our interest in each other,
however — and I met and started acting
with and got hung up on Martha.

Martha was Gigi, in a stage adaptation
of Colette's short novel. I was her suitor,
Gaston, the male lead (Maurice Chevalier's
part didn't exist in the original drama). We
even had a love scene. But Martha and I
started making eyes at each other even
before the first rehearsal, meeting at parties
of course, me surprised at her interest but
eager — she radiated such pure, intelligent
sexuality — to take advantage of it. But
classically, as my interest increased (expo-
nentially) hers diminished, and I was left
with our rehearsed love scenes only and a

growing bitterness, anguish, agony, sexual need. "Me outside with a hammer at the doorbell," according to a song I wrote at the time.

I was still a virgin. I was very unsure of the way of the world, and wanted in on the secret.

I was singing the blues.

Relationships with women/relationships with men. I was much more interested in the former that year, but since I wasn't actually actively pursuing Judy, Bill and I were able to go on enjoying our old friendship, with just kind of an exciting edge added to it by his awareness of my ambiguous relationship with his girlfriend.

I knew as little about it as he did. By early February he and I were both just sort of waiting for some kind of signal from her; and then I was over at her apartment one day, talking with her and her mother about nothing much, and then back in her room she turned on me suddenly and said, with real viciousness, "Well, if you think that *I'm* going to make a decision — !" I should have taken her in my arms, tried to ease her obvious pain. It was an expression of love for me as much as anything, but it caught me by surprise, I was scared. I did what I thought was the honorable thing: I told Bill a few days later that the field was his.

A lot of things contributed to my decision: one was Martha, of course — she had already entered my sphere of awareness at this point. Another was Judy herself: I wanted her but I was afraid of her, too — sometimes she'd look so hard and efficient, and also there were moments when our inability to communicate seemed so total that I really despaired of what would happen if all the complications were gone and it was just her and me together alone.

And Sara: she and Judy had been friends, rivals, and she would resent a continuing relationship between me and Judy in her absence far more than any affair I might have with some other woman.

But most of all I think it was my relationship with Bill, and my unwillingness to violate that relationship by competing openly for the lady's hand, that tipped the balance. And a lack of self-confidence: I was quite aware that I might lose such a competition, in which case I would have lost not one but both of them. No Judy *and* no Bill . . . it was too bleak a prospect. I was a coward. I let him have her.

And then he went on *his* trip to Europe, early that summer, and for one brief shining moment, just before Sara returned from England, Judy and I got together again.

I dropped by her house and we went

for a walk, near the river, at night; we
stopped, and kissed, tongue tip touching
tongue tip for less than an instant, and a
spark jumped between us that shattered the
heavens.

I walked her home, saw her the next
day, and then that was that for the next
few years. But those two days were like a
lifetime.

X.

Paul, you're incredible. You crack me up, sitting there at your typewriter waiting for me to talk to you, drinking white wine and cold coffee alternately in little sips, listening to (and thinking about) Neil Young, occasionally taking hits of grass from a cheap wooden pipe purchased from a street vendor at 42nd Street and Lexington Avenue.

Is this your idea of a seance?

Well, if I'm a spirit of the dead, I guess you've called me up. (Same system I used to use after a deadline day, or tripping: ring twice, hang up, then call again and I'll answer.) But what's a "spirit," and where is "dead"? These words are easy to use; but I wonder if you've ever really thought about what they mean.

I'm gone, you think, and therefore I can't be here speaking these words, and so this is either fabrication or else some kind of mystery or magic.

Yeah, except for one thing: I'm not gone.

It's so simple. It's like, energy distribution. Being alive is just one of many states that consciousness can and does take. The Law of Conservation of Energy — which applies during the shift from one state to another, like when I died — could also be called the Law of Continuity of Consciousness.

I'm not gone.

Neither is anyone else who ever lived. As the discovery of DNA/RNA suggests, the information-recording abilities of living organisms, including homo sapiens, are extraordinary. It's our information *retrieval* abilities that are so limited, so unevolved. The whole history of our species, in impossible detail, is available in every cell of every living brain; but our conscious minds lack access to most of that history, simply because we haven't yet learned how to read our own minds. (I'll give you a clue: it can't be done with a knife.)

So Paul, I guess I'm speaking to you not so much from the spirit world as from inside one of your own brain cells.

Hello out there.

LSD = the ever expanding moment. Which is another form of time, and equally valid: our lives perceived as a succession of acid trips, or shall we

                                         Paul Williams

say, "moments of intensity," with all the months and years in between null and void. The expanding moment is, in this time-system, the only real one, the only place where anything really happens.

The rush of acceleration is terrifying. It's like feeling the Gs when a space ship takes off: can you stand the pressure, and don't you want to panic when you feel it increasing every moment? How can I possibly ride this wave?

Paul and I looked at each other across what might have been surfboards on the crest of a monstrous wave rising by Diamond Head but was actually just the bed in my Bleecker Street loft. That first taste of the trip is so delicious that I could never feel anxious. Paul would look at me with wonder and fear in his eyes, such mixed emotions; I dug his excitement, and he in turn seemed to thrive on my sense of calm.

We looked at each other and talked with each other, as the moment got larger and larger, and I know before we got out the other side that some kind of mitosis took place.

Our minds got together and absorbed each other and split apart again. I've been in Paul's mind ever since, and he was in mine till I died. I have other locations, too, of course; the rule for survival is, *diversify*. This process of diversification, which is as they say asexual, is as important in the evolution of species as the genetic diversification that results from sexual reproduction.

Any time two people are in each other's

presence, this asexual intercourse occurs. The more intense the contact, of course, the more we absorb and are absorbed. It is at the same time the most normal and most special of all occurrences. In this act, far more than in the act of parenthood, lies our immortality as individuals.

It is our friends, our enemies, and our lovers who give us eternal life.

I'm searching for the heart of gold at the end of the rainbow. It's like the picture of the cube that goes in and out as you shift your eyes and your assumptions. An M.C. Escher print, all positive and negative: blink your eyes, and the story of my life, any life, is the story of failure after failure after failure. Blink again, and it's a thousand small and/or glorious victories.

Up is the shadow of down. Light can be defined as the temporary absence of darkness, and so on *ad nauseam* all around our peripheral vision. Are these zigzags white teeth on a black background, or black teeth on white? Never mind; the important thing is, it's not a dichotomy. Shadow and light are inevitably paired simply because they are in fact the same thing, seen edgewise, rising and falling at the same time.

In the long year 1965, Paul failed at love again and again. He started the year with three beautiful prospects; by December he had exhausted all of them, and himself, and somehow found nothing new even after four months on a coeducational college campus. What he found, indeed, was an ever-growing emptiness inside himself, a primal doubt he'd never expected to have to confront: will I ever be loved? Is it *possible* to love me? Or am I in fact cursed, unable to give or receive, condemned to an eternity of watching those other happy souls dance at a distance?

Oh, woe is me. But the thing is, there is a delicious satisfaction in all that romantic unfulfillment. Failure is success, light and shadow, and so 1965 was the year Paul found love, found it far more than the year before when he first met and felt attracted to both Sara and Judy, found it with the sort of agony and joy (to musical accompaniment) that makes us all true believers, and insures that we will never give up the search. Paul succeeded at his greatest endeavor that year, which was achieving a romantic view of himself, despite his middle-class roots and surroundings. For someone else, it might have come naturally, easily; but Paul had to work at it, swimming bold against all the tides of his intellect, and even with all that unrequited love he just barely made it. Society welcomed this honor student, this National Merit Scholar, with open arms. But the ladies spurned him — they saw something in his energy just a little too unstable, unpleasant, dangerous & pushy, without the saving grace of real animal beauty — they wouldn't give him comfort when he needed it most, and maybe that's what saved his soul.

After I died, I got to know Paul a lot better than I ever had in our lifetime. I just watched, observed — participated, if you will — but with a detachment and an interest I could never have achieved while living, death set me free from my obsession with myself and my own little plans and responsibilities, left me unencumbered and able for the first time to throw my entire attention to the riddle of the human creature and what he does with his life.

I watched Paul. I watched him and I saw myself, but I saw a whole lot more, too, a lot of things that I'd never noticed about him or me or anyone. I saw the way he moved — I mean over a period of months and years, the way he moved around on the planet, his pattern, his message. I saw him go back and forth between the East Coast and the West Coast, for example, again and again — and I realized he was like a bee, one of a million buzzing bees aiding the the cultural cross-pollination. And then I saw that I'd been something like that, too, and that I could continue to be, if I wanted, even though I was "dead."

The world is populated, not by living bodies, but by living spirits. I live. I feel. I am a spirit, telling you this story, and if you look you'll see spirits everywhere.

Here is a chart of Paul's travels in the two years after my death:

Aug/Sept '68: New York to Berkeley and
    Mendocino, back to New York
Oct '68: New York to Mendocino
Nov '68: Mendocino to Berkeley & back
Dec '68: to Los Angeles and back
Jan '69: to San Francisco and back
Feb/March '69: to Los Angeles, then
    New York
April '69: back to Mendocino
May/June '69: to San Francisco, San Luis
    Obispo, Miami, New York, Montreal,
    Bennington, Martha's Vineyard,
    Boston, New York, Mendocino
Aug/Sept '69: to Woodstock Festival,
    Boston, New York, back to Men-
    docino
Oct '69: to Hayward, Calif — Big Sur —
    back to Mendocino
Nov/Dec '69: to Seattle — British Co-
    lumbia — back to Mendocino
Jan/March '70: to San Francisco, New
    York, Boston, Vermont, Arkansas, New
    York, Vermont, Mendocino
April '70: to Vancouver, then Lund,
    British Columbia
May '70: to Apple Bay, British Columbia
(his movements were restricted to a
20-mile radius for the next 7 months)

You are familiar with "slow motion" tech-
niques. There is also "fast motion." When I look at

these years of Paul's life in "fast motion," I see his
movements as a single line — not a blur at all but
a clear and graceful expression of something he
could scarcely have been aware of — let's call it
The Force. There are a thousand manifestations of
The Force visible in any cross-section of any of our
lives — a day, a year, a minute. We are in motion
all the time, and every motion is a message, a
song, a painting, a piece of coded information. I
look at Paul and try to receive his messages. I
wasn't too good at it at first, but I'm learning
every day.

I wonder who's looking at me.

XI.

On April 30th, 1966, Richard Fariña died in a
motorcycle accident. Paul, who had talked with
Fariña, listened to his music, printed an article of
his (in the third *Crawdaddy!*, March '66), and
waited impatiently for his book to be published,
acted like he'd been hit by a lightning bolt. It was
his first death. He refused to believe the news at
first, spent long hours trying to contact people
who could confirm or deny, meanwhile offering
himself (and the gathered friends who knew Fariña
or had listened to his music) persuasive arguments
that the fragment of radio news someone had
heard could well have been misunderstood or
untrue.

And when the feared confirmation came,
Paul became obsessed with the need to react, just

sitting around feeling sad together wasn't enough
— he decided he would go to California (where
he had never been) to attend the funeral. And
how would he get there? Easy — he'd go to the
airport and hitch a ride on a freight plane. He'd
talked to several people who claimed to have
done this — the story was, certain pilots would let
you ride in the cockpit with them, figuring no one
would ever find out unless you crashed, in which
case you and he didn't care any more anyway.

Paul admitted that the plan was a little far-
fetched, but he'd just go to the airport and try it
and if he couldn't get a ride, well, okay. One of his
friends — she'd spent some time with Dick and
Mimi at the Institute for the Study of Nonviolence,
in Carmel — got a car somehow and drove him to
Philadelphia International Airport. They sat together awhile on a bench in a waiting room —
held each other — and parted. It was six in the
morning, and she had to get back to the campus.

Paul wandered around. Before arriving, he'd
had a mental image of the sort of place freight
pilots would hang out — a little coffee shop, or
bar, somewhere "backstage" at the airport. After
all, there was a place for the passengers; there had
to be somewhere for the other side to go, too.

But he had no idea how to find that place.
Paul was not very experienced with airports —
he'd been in a lot of different ones during his
month in the Soviet Union, but his only air trip
inside the U.S. had been the flight from Boston to

Swarthmore and back when he visited the college
as a high school student.

　He tried to talk to a stewardess, but she
couldn't understand what it was he wanted to
know. Then he walked through an unmarked door
from the terminal, and found himself in a large
passageway, long blank walls painted light blue,
some kind of service area — he decided to see
where it went.

All he knew was he had to get to that
funeral — Dick was dead and Paul had to *do*
something . . . He walked along in a half-daze and
was met by an airport security cop who immediately ordered him back against the wall, hands
over his head. Paul had encountered plenty of
cops on his hitchhiking adventures, but this guy
really meant business. After he frisked Paul, he told
him to stand there without moving, and called a
city cop on his radio. The city cops came, ques-
tioned Paul, listened to his outrageous explanation
of what he was doing there, and then told him
they were booking him for trespassing on airport
property. On the way to the station house in Philly
itself, Paul was told they had to take him in to see
the guy in charge of juveniles, since he'd been
turned over to them by airport security — Paul
was less than a month shy of his eighteenth birthday — but that the charge would almost surely be
dropped after questioning in Philly, since they
didn't have enough space in the jails to hold
people for something like "trespassing."

Okay. They got into center city, and Paul was interviewed in the middle of a large room in the station house by a 250-pound "juvenile assistance officer" named Officer Sheehan. It was quiet, early morning, maybe one or two other cops around. Officer Sheehan wanted to know how Paul was doing at school, what courses he was taking . . . He was particularly interested in the fact that Paul had a class in *Chinese* history (one of the few classes Paul hadn't quit going to already; it had been a dull, unsatisfying semester academically). Upon learning that Paul wasn't absolutely certain he would return to college next September, the officer asked him if he wanted to join the Army (May 1966; the draft calls were getting larger every month). Paul, thinking the wrong answer could land him in a recruiting office, said no, he didn't want to join the Army.

"Why not?"

"Well, uh, I don't know . . . You see, uh, sir, I guess I don't entirely approve of what we're doing over there — "

WHAM! "I *thought* you were one of those ..." says Officer Sheehan, as he simultaneously belts our boy in the face.

Paul was knocked backwards. The punch broke his glasses, knocked them to the floor. The officer started coming at him, and Paul started screaming, threats and invective: "You mother-fucking bastard, I'm going to get you for that, you'll lose your job, I'm going to — "

                                    Paul Williams

Another policeman came over; he dragged
Paul to a temporary cell in the back of the room
while Officer Sheehan returned Paul's threats with
interest. Then the two men went to confer, leaving Paul in the cell with a black teenager who said
he was being held as a runaway but wouldn't talk
after that, he had no energy or desire even to look
up. Paul paced around the cell — an empty room
with a barred door — checked out the toilet,
looked out into the main room, tried to think . . .
But what can you think about in a situation like
that? Only two things: "How did I get here?", and
"How do I get out?"

After awhile they came and moved Paul to
another temporary cell in the same building, a
tiny room with a cot. He didn't know it yet, but he
had been charged with assaulting a police officer.
A felony.

Paul was busted for his age, as much as anything. He was seventeen. When he'd arrived at the
station house he'd asked to make a phone call and
was refused — "minors have no rights." (This was
before the courts started reinterpreting that particular wrinkle). Then the police themselves called
his mother and explained the situation, letting
Paul talk to her for just a moment. They wanted to
find out if he was a runaway. He wasn't, of course;
he was a college student; but his mother hedged.
She was worried about her son, she knew he had a
tendency to act rashly and if he was so upset by

his friend's death, wouldn't he go right back to trying to get to California as soon as the police let him go? She asked them to hold Paul there until she could get to Philadelphia.

A half hour later, Paul had his interview with Officer Sheehan.

Paul sat in his cell, with his broken glasses, waiting for his mother to arrive from Boston and wondering what was going to happen next. Eventually he fell asleep, for the first time in 28 hours. Then they woke him up, and put him in a van with a dozen other juveniles, and drove him across the city to some kind of house of detention.

He didn't stay there long. It was one of those no-room-at-the-inn situations — he and the others sat on benches in a waiting room for an hour or so, and then all but a few were herded into another van (bars on the windows) and taken to another jail or reformatory where again they waited in vain. This went on all day and well into the evening — once Paul was put in a cell with six or seven of his traveling companions, but that didn't last — somewhere along the way he heard the new Rolling Stones single for the first time (it was "Paint It Black") on a radio in another room.

Eventually, because the city jails were all full, no room for juveniles or adults, he ended up at the nearest branch of the Pennsylvania State Prison. Now, this place usually caters to your more hardened breed of criminal, but what the hell —

they put him through the regular routine, along
with several dozen other recent arrivals: strip, get
a number band and wear it around your arm,
shower, put on regulation sweat pants and shirt,
go to be photographed. The photographer looked
at Paul and said, "Boy, you're going to get a
haircut — real soon!"

It was 1966. Hair was an issue. Vietnam was
an issue. LSD was becoming an issue, ever since
the cover story in *Life Magazine*. (Paul hadn't taken
any yet. He'd started wearing his hair a little
longer, just letting it grow, about a year earlier, on
the advice of his director when he was acting in
Gigi — she said she'd write a note to the headmaster of Paul's school, if necessary, explaining that his
hair had to be longer for his part in the play . . .
After the play was finished the headmaster hinted
broadly several times that it was time for a trim;
but Paul was by then a second semester senior,
and he paid no attention to the hints. Which fits
in with my theory that it was the young *women*
who decided young men would start wearing long
hair . . .) Americans were starting to get suspi-
cious of anyone under thirty. The word "hippie"
had not yet been invented, but hair was certainly
a signal —

At this point Paul (who had been sleepwalking through the whole episode up till now)
surprised himself by getting the attention of some
sort of authority figure, deep in the underground
reaches of Penn State Priz, and telling him that he

did not want his hair cut. Paul insisted to the man that he was only going to be there that night, that it was a mistake that he was there at all and that it would be corrected first thing in the morning: "If I do come back tomorrow night then you can cut my hair or do whatever you want, isn't that right? You don't have to do it now . . . " He was suddenly energetic, defending his hair, his autonomy, and when he saw he was winning his case he added an urgent request for a solitary cell for his one night there — he knew what he was in for otherwise, as a seventeen-year-old college student with a virgin asshole . . .

They didn't cut off his hair ("Hey, how'd you get away with *that?*" asked a fellow prisoner, and Paul answered honestly, "I don't know") and eventually they even gave him a cell alone, after first assigning him to one with two guys already in it. The night passed uneventfully. But it was strange waking up before dawn, wondering where he was, and then remembering . . .

They took him to the courthouse in the morning — street clothes again — his mother was there and they sat together in court, waiting to be called for a hearing. The hearing turned out to be a private interview with a judge or judge's assistant, and it was at this point that Paul first found out that he'd been charged with assaulting a police officer. "It's a felony, ma'am, and we can't release him before the trial — " "When is that?" "A week from today." "But you can't keep him in *prison* for a week . . . " "We have no choice."

She wouldn't take no for an answer, and eventually, in another tribute to the persuasiveness of the Williamses, or maybe just to the implicit power of the white middle class, they released him, put him in her custody until the trial. Paul thought this ironic, since without her he wouldn't have been in there, but he was glad to get out.

Wind whistles across the page. Do you know of any blanks in your memory? Have you looked lately? Paul and I are writing this story by zeroing in on people and events in his recent life, as recorded in his memory. Odd place, the memory. You don't know what's there till you look for it, and it's always possible to look a little closer. Mostly we just grab at the obvious stuff, the bigger chunks, figuring that must be what's important.

Then, as we write, we have to look deeper into Paul's mind to get the *details* of the story . . . that's when things get a little rough sometimes. We run into blank spots. Wind whistles across the page, the clean sheet of paper in the typewriter laughs at us as we wrack our memory, Paul's memory, thinking, "What happened next? What happened?"

Oh, the essentials are there, the frame: we know Paul and his mother found a lawyer, we know they went back to Belmont for a week and then returned for their day in court. Grabbing ahold of sufficient details to tell the courtroom story is no problem. But there are other likely stories that seem to have gotten away. Paul can't remember how he and his mother got back to Belmont — by plane? Or did she drive up from Boston in the first place, is that why it took her so long to get there? Did they visit Swarthmore to pick up clothes or tell the dean why Paul wouldn't be around for the next week (at least)? Did they fight, in the car (or the plane — less likely)? Did they even talk? There are parts of Paul's privacy I penetrate with ease, and other parts that seem to hide from me . . . and maybe from him. Unpleasant experiences, sure. But why unpleasant, and in what way? Unpleasant because they manifestly tell him things he doesn't want to know about himself, little jolts of self-realization? Oh that face in the mirror . . .

Maybe those missing memories are just trivial details, hard to find because they weren't considered important enough to keep in the active file. It's possible. But I doubt it. I'm not saying Paul should exert himself to try to recapture those moments — that would be an inappropriate response. But I think he should be aware that the blank spots are there.

Paul and his mother returned to Philadelphia by train and spent a long (impatient) day waiting for Paul's case to come up in juvenile court. Six hours past the appointed time, the case was called.

Officer Sheehan was there with the lieutenant who'd helped him subdue Paul. Sheehan took the stand first, and testified that he'd been talking with the defendant when suddenly defendant jumped up and socked him, knocking him across the room. The lieutenant testified that what Officer Sheehan had said was indeed true. Paul's lawyer asked the lieutenant some questions that got him a little tangled up, and then the judge called a recess.

Paul had no idea what was going on. The judge — who seemed to Paul to be someone who might understand his story, perhaps just because he was black — talked with Paul's lawyer privately for fifteen or twenty minutes. Then he reconvened the court, and announced that he was going to dismiss the case on the grounds that his court didn't have jurisdiction — he said that since Paul was a minor, and a resident of Massachusetts, the two cops would have to go to Massachusetts if they wanted to press assault charges against him. Sheehan turned red and started arguing, but his partner shut him up. As they left the courthouse, the lawyer explained to Paul and his mother that, although it's a pretty serious thing to stand in court charged with assaulting an officer with just your word against a policeman who has a witness, the cops made a tactical error when Sheehan and then his friend claimed that Paul had knocked Sheehan across the room. The judge looked from the 250-pound policeman to the 120-pound kid, and back, and realized he couldn't convict Paul. The lawyer admitted that even he began to believe his client's story at that point.

But the judge had a problem. This was juvenile court; Officer Sheehan was a (ahem) juvenile assistance officer, kind of a counselor and a specialist; the point was, in order not to convict Paul the judge would have to directly or indirectly call the two policemen liars, and this is not good practice, especially when you're dealing with officers who are in and out of your court every week of the year. So the answer was for the judge not to rule on the case, yet make it practically impossible for the officers to press their charges. The judge and lawyer huddled, figured out how to do that, and called it a day. The lawyer earned $500.

A fair price for freedom. But one of the clear lessons of the day was, if you can afford a lawyer, okay; if not, forget it. You don't walk out of juvenile court just because your story is true. Not in Philly in '66, anyway.

And you don't get free in this world just by walking out of a courthouse. Within minutes, Paul and his mother were screaming at each other; the release of one set of tensions brought other tensions to the fore. They screamed on the street and people turned and watched; both of them wanted liberation, she from the oppression of felt responsibility, he from the oppression of outside authority. He didn't want to talk with her, and that infuriated her; both of them felt that the other had gotten

     Paul Williams

him/her into this mess, and neither had any capacity or energy left to see things from the other's point of view. For Paul's part, he felt — though he couldn't have articulated it — that offering her any information about his life, his feelings about his life and what he was going to do at this point, would be tantamount to letting her look over his shoulder and kibitz while he made a series of extremely tough and personal decisions. Impossible. In his turmoil, she was the last person in the world he could talk to — she more than anyone else was the person whose worldview he had to stay clear of in order to give his own fragile worldview a chance to function properly.

And see how the fates rule our lives? Paul made his decision, he'd made the only decision he could make during the week between his arrest and his trial — it was the second week in May, exams were ten days away, Paul had been refusing to confront the situation (he needed four credits to complete his freshman year, he had kept up with none of his courses and had already been booted out of one, leaving him short one credit even if he put on the old impossible burst of energy and studied round the clock for several weeks before exams — he knew he could do it, but he also knew that he didn't *want* to do it, and that was a factor he hadn't had to consider in high school) back before the death and the bust, but now . . . Now he had lost another nine days, and any feeling for college in general and Swarthmore in particular that he might ever have had. Things had just come to a head. If he hadn't been busted at the airport, if he hadn't been held at the police station in Philly, he might have tried to go through with it, come back to school, do some last minute cramming and talking to profs, take the exams and somehow stick the semester together with scotch tape and promises. It can be done, it's been done a million times. *Crawdaddy!* was not on his mind at this point, not much had happened after the third issue came out in March and it was starting to seem like a dead end, no response. Paul's big problem was that he had nowhere to go and no sense of himself as a person apart from the school or home environment. He was confused, he was stuck. Fariña's death and the incredible, irrelevant tangle with the Philly cops had effectively, in his head or gut, ended all chances of his faking his way through the semester, maybe just by waking him up to the confusion in his life, to the fact that he could no longer fake anything. He left his mother screaming on the street in Philadelphia and went to the campus, went to the dean and told him he wanted to withdraw from the semester. The dean told him it was weeks too late to do that — which meant he'd have to fail, and then wait a year before readmission. And then in the next breath the dean said he'd make an exception, and so Paul withdrew from the second semester of his freshman year. And kissed Swarthmore goodbye.

 Paul Williams

XII.

These in order any words are not.

I Donald John McNeill do solemnly swear that I am writing this book just as sure as you're reading it. If you can feel me, I exist. I think it's as simple as that.

How many people out there can still *feel*, even in these rough times? Hold up your hands, folks. Okay, officer, arrest them.

Paul went back to Cambridge and moved in with a saint. What other word is there for a man who gladly shares his one-room apartment for six months with an eighteen-year-old boy who pays nothing toward the rent and in whom he has no sexual interest? Paul lived on one side of the room, in and on a bed that had previously been covered with magazines and books; Larry lived on the other side, on a sort of square double bed higher than Paul's and therefore in another world. The two kept different hours, and maintained a good sense of mutual privacy. It was relatively rare for both of them to be in the room awake at the same time.

It was a great thing that Larry did, giving Paul that bit of space. Paul knew that if he tried to live at home, with his mother, he'd go off the deep end. But he had very little alternative — he had no money, and little chance of finding a job. He could do some free-lance work (proofreading, copy editing), but not enough to be able to pay rent somewhere. And then Larry offered him the use of the spare bed . . .

Paul's life went through some rapid and needed changes.

part two

XIII.

What I should really do, I think, is start writing the second part of *Heart of Gold*. At first this second part may seem to bear little resemblance to the first, but if you just hang in there we always manage to slop the loose ends together somehow.

I think Don mentioned that some months before he died he got into this thing of getting stoned alone and staring into mirrors. I remember he reported to me, in his usual low-key fashion, about how scary and fascinating this could be. Like some kind of forbidden game, the danger being that you might find out something you'd rather not know, might release some demon that couldn't be pushed back through the glass. Don found these encounters unpleasant but also somewhat addictive.

Who are we? Do we really want to know? The latter question is the interesting one, this is a book not about the story of my life but rather about the stories of our lives, I'm interested in examining what we think those stories are, what do we say when asked, what do we tell ourselves?

I know that in my heart of hearts my own sexual history is more important to me than the names of the books I've written. But staring in the mirror stoned my body disappears and all I can see are those eyes. There's something alive back there. Fifteen minutes on and I'm in the sorcerer's universe, dealing with forces I'm truly not trained to confront. Is this related to dreams that confuse themselves with real events of the day before and the morning after? I don't really like this ambiguity, there's something sinister about it, and yet it's quite a thrill. Give me more but keep it safe, okay? No, let's just forget the whole thing. Mmm . . .

"I'll be your mirror/reflect what you are . . . " Fucking is the only form of this confrontation I truly feel comfortable with, the only mirror game wholesome enough (when love's involved, an affair of the heart)

                    Paul Williams

to give myself up to, let go, relax, break
through, *become visible* to the other side.
I want you. No sacrifice too great.

Let me in, damn it. We have to complete this connection.

And the mirrors seem so sterile by
contrast, I mean a sheet of silvered glass,
no lips for my tongue to find, no arms
around conscious bodies pressing, pulling
us closer together. Is this just self-hypno-
sis? I don't want any part of it, I'd rather
feel homesick lust for every beautiful being
in the universe.

I'd rather walk straight into darkness.

And yet there's this fascination, we
wonder what happens after death, as
though we existed apart from the embrace,
and yes I suppose we do. Though incom-
pletely, some sort of half-creature, floating,
forlorn, blissed out no doubt and self-contained but always desperate for fusion.

And we think if we see ourselves in
mirrors we'll get a clue. Some kind of solip-
sism. Dangerous, like staring into the sun.
I'm glad you're reading these words I'm
writing. This would be insanity if I were
here all alone.

I think I'll try again now. It's June 3d,
1977, same day I wrote the above, which
already I only half understand. If I look at

myself alone in the mirror I see nothing,
I think that's the idea, for any real insight
I have to look at myself as I'm seen by
other people. It's a year and a half since
work on part one halted in mid-flow, and
I'm starting to think it's no coincidence the
story stopped just before I was to lose my
virginity.

Language constantly fails us. And yet a
fellow like me, driven by whatever internal
pressure, survives to write again. This is
not the most lovely prose I've ever committed to paper, and yet the important thing is
it's coming forth, there's a chance I'm starting to slip around whatever obstruction I
placed in my path.

The passage of time is fascinating.
Between you and me, it's nonexistent. I stop
and start, you stop and start, and neither of
us knows the difference. In this way we
differ from lovers, who touch each other at
the same time, who require (for the dura-
tion of the act) each other's more or less
uninterrupted attention. My friend Don
McNeill, now discorporate, has a perspective on time (if we admit his existence) all-
but-incomprehensible to you and me. Time
doesn't pass for him; he sits outside and
watches. Or so I imagine. If he and I were
lovers now, how would we relate to each
other?

Dear Paul, very funny question. Before when I helped you with this book, we were working towards a weekly deadline, three and a half pages delivered to Soho by subway every Friday. I felt good about that. It gave some shape to the project.

Oh Paul, how do you remember who I am? And what does it mean, because I'm not that memory any more, I'm someone else, no way you could see it but I've gone through my changes too. Do you hear me? I want to keep caring about the planet I was born on, but it's hard to make these long distance phone calls. Paul!

Yes, Don. It's good to hear your voice —

Paul, I'm so far away I don't know where I am. But it's only a problem of language. The distance between us is nothing two lovers couldn't enclose painlessly if only they knew how — I guess I'm saying it takes practice. A problem of motivation. Once people like you and me had to figure out how to transport themselves across bodies of water; they invented boats. All kinds of boats. If you hear me, I'm saying, "create a vehicle."

Become a sailboat. Turn your face to the wind and the sun.

XIV.

I want to say hello to all my friends on Earth. In another world you're dead and I'm alive, but in all the possibilities we were separated. This sadness is at the heart of our history — and sometimes I don't see it as a sadness at all, just a beautiful source of light.

(Our lives are paintings. Look for where the light is coming from, the source of the illumination.)

I feel so much love for all of you — I felt so much love for you when we were alive together, too, but it wasn't always possible to say so. Isn't it interesting that that's such a difficult thing? I want to apologize for not telling you while I had the chance; but you know some part of me was *trying* to tell you every moment that we were together.

And thank you too, dear friends, for whatever you felt then. It didn't go unnoticed.

Look, Don, I can't go through with this. I've been staring at the next bunch of paragraphs you dictated through me, and I like them fine, for themselves. But I am made awful uncomfortable by what they lead to. You've got me set up to talk about a certain person, how we met, who she seemed to me and how we changed and stayed connected. Nice story. But I'm not ready, you know I don't like to tell any kind of straight-line story, scares the hell out of me. And no matter how you set this up, I have to feel like I'm the one who's doing the work, "I did this and then she & he did that," squeezing my memory for details like an old toothpaste tube with holes in three places. If you could just make it all flood out of my unconscious and onto the typewritten page, well okay, I'm sure I could live with it. But short of that, please understand, it's too much awkward effort, I can't help it I just have to draw the line.

For one thing, dear friend, I really don't know what you felt. I found out that first weekend I spent with Helen, after you had me take her to the Chuck Berry concert and virtually precipitated us into bed with each other, that you were in love with her, had

asked her more than once to marry you.
Well I was fascinated by this added touch of
intimacy of course — while we were together she had a dream about you, in which
the two of you *were* married — but I had no
idea what either of you really felt about
each other or why you hadn't walked down
the aisle or even made love long since, I
still don't know and one unfairness of this
collaboration is that while you can walk
around in my mind and memories, I can't
get close to yours. I know love's a mystery
of course and endlessly fascinating in all its
disguises but here, just look at these words
you wrote:

> Eyes are windows. Windows suggest
> one is outside or inside. Windows stand
> between. The eyes of women and the
> eyes of men are half-mirrors, like the
> surfaces of a body of water. Looking
> from without or within, our vision is di-
> vided: part penetration, part reflection.
> I only partially see you. The rest of
> what I'm seeing is me.
> I introduced Paul to my friend Helen.
> I . . . well, I saw a similarity in them,
> they reminded me of each other so
> much I just had to see what would
> happen if they got together.
> They seduced each other right away.

Okay. But now you sit silent, waiting for me to speak. And I don't know what to say. My relationship with Helen — Lark — is such a confusion over the years, I still don't know what was happening half the time and neither does she I'm sure. It just slides around, sometimes she's angry at me or I'm angry at her, most of the time we don't speak the same language and yet we still have this mutual attraction, loyalty, love and a helpless sense of mixed destinies, if only for all the close friends and life-situations we, despite great separations, have in common. Starting with you, Don. But to narrate the details of my collision with this headstrong and breathtaking Sagittarian female seems now an invasion of intimacy, despite the true stories we managed to tell together in part one of this manuscript I find myself with the hesitation blues here, we haven't found our vehicle yet. How to tell a story? She loved you, that much was always clear to me, but she didn't find you sexually attractive. What does it mean, how can such things be? I wouldn't tell this truth to anyone who still had a body. Too cruel and frustrating, this twist between love and sexual attraction has never made sense to me, half the time I don't even believe it, definitely a case of God's inexplicable torture, as in the Book of Job. And so you introduced her and me. We fucked like rabbits (sometimes) but never, as far as I know, entertained any thoughts of being mates. It was a brother-and-sister type connection, and perhaps at first we were even using each other as surrogates for you. I can see you smile at the thought. I think it's horrible, where is the justice? But you always had a more serene outlook, kinder than the rest of us it seemed and more able to see the joke. Anyway I don't want to talk about any of this. If eyes are windows, then all I want to know is: when will I see you again?

Dear Paul: you're seeing me now.

Every one of us has a story, a sequence of stories; sweep past our minds for a moment and don't you see how naked we are at heart? We *want* to be seen, this is the closely-guarded secret, every "I" inwardly knows itself to be beautiful and waits for those loving eyes that will see and create this truth. My story = me. Every one of us tells her story, his story, every moment, fearing and praying that someone less deaf and blind than all the others will have eyes to see and ears to hear.

My friend, at age eighteen just barely, was visited in his Cambridge room by the girl, woman, he'd been seeing for the past few weeks. She came to tell him goodbye: two years older, already burned by love, she felt they were getting too close for comfort and she just didn't want to be misunderstood. She didn't like the way he pushed sometimes. He was surprised and hurt, he really cared for her, he accepted her news and just let go, told his story & let his loneliness shine, it made her feel so tender towards him she cradled him in her arms, he held her and though it wasn't his plan he couldn't help it, just had to try one last time to make love to her. And his need was so great, she feeling so vulnerable after each had revealed herself/himself so generously to the other, she let him go through with it; it wasn't very pleasurable love-making and later she felt that he'd forced her, she told him so, it wasn't very pleasurable but still his body did enter her body, and for him it was the first time.

They stayed friends, saw each other and grew closer in some ways but when they were in bed together her hostility to him as a male wanting sex was more than he could bear or overcome. When she left Cambridge to go visit her parents for the rest of the summer, he felt mixed emotions. Their friendship, though stormy, had truly been a friendship; and their sex — well, sex as a struggle was a bitter, humiliating experience, but it was an experience Paul couldn't regret. He was sorry that it all seemed to be so difficult, but still he was glad he'd crossed the line.

There were other women, not many, scattered moments as the months went by. No steady relationships — he wrote to the woman who'd ended his virginity, and saw her again once on a hitchhiking trip to the midwest, but nothing had changed and they still weren't lovers even though they liked each other and had once made love. In December Paul moved to New York, after a while he even had his own apartment, he made love to a few women who failed to inspire him once the horniness was satisfied (and, oh, that's an awkward and painful feeling! it really was love, lovesex, he wanted, and he felt like a weak damn fool when mere horniness could push him around) and he got a huge crush on a beauty from his former college who wouldn't make love to him and soon stopped seeing him because he wanted too much. So he slowly gained sexual experience, but never got love-satisfaction, not till more than a year had passed and it was summer again, July '67. He met Jeanne, fell in love with her, saw her every day and experienced his first true sexual relationship, loving and joyous and fiercely intense. It was magnificent. It very nearly killed him.

I can't tell you about Paul and Jeanne without first offering a few vague impressions of who Paul had become by the summer of '67. He had become a friend of mine, for one thing; now we're dealing with that part of the time span where Paul and I knew each other and were friends and were both alive and in the same universe. He was working hard, editing a magazine which was his own invention but now very much the property also of

its readers and the other people who wrote for it
and worked on it, he was the boss and he was
under a lot of pressure, dealing with people, but
he was also flying high with the success and excitement of it all. He was very excited by the
music still, and the energy rising all around us.
He'd gotten involved with the hip community —
and he'd met me — as a result of a phone call
from a guy named Jim Fouratt, who invited him to
take part in plans for a New York Be-In. He was
smoking marijuana — first tasted it in September
'66 in Cambridge, first got off and got into it in
December, visiting L.A. — and taking acid, big
doses, no holds barred. He was writing. He was
traveling. In truth, he was exploding. Fouratt
introduced him to Jeanne Evans — she needed a
job, he needed a managing editor. She was smart,
tough, experienced. She was also momentarily
unattached, and tremendously attractive. Paul
worked with Jeanne for a week, then went to
Toronto and Montreal (the Airplane and the Dead
were bringing psychedelia to Canada, and Paul
went along as a journalist and a fan) and thought
about Jeanne all the time and came back and
went out with her for a night on the town
(Country Joe at the Cafe Au Go-Go, Hendrix at the
Scene) and they talked and talked and ended up
at her apartment, he still shy, finally she said "Are
you going to spend the night?" and he melted.
Their passion that night was phenomenal, and it
grew more intense by the day. She was nine years

                    Paul Williams

older than him. They loved each other, they played like children. He was in heaven. He couldn't believe it.

Working together was tough, was tense, they were both strong-willed, he'd hired her to take away some of the incredible weight of his own responsibility, but he had no idea how to delegate authority, the only way he knew to get things done was to worry about everything all the time, he looked over her shoulder and quarreled with her till she wanted to strangle him. She loved him at night and hated him in the day. It was getting to be a strained relationship.

Jeanne was starting to wonder how long she could stand it. But Paul was blinded; she was the love of his life, it was the first time he'd ever lived with somebody, their world together was a thousand times richer than anything he'd ever experienced, three weeks after they'd gotten together life without her was literally inconceivable.

He held her like he'd never let go.

We live with others half-consciously at best; and perhaps it's true that the more we feel, the more we love, the less we see. We are blinded not only to the other's faults but, more importantly, to our own. In lovers' eyes we see ourselves at our best, and the joy of such an experience is heady brew indeed. But the very intensity of the interaction between two people in love and sharing all time and space together means that in lovers' eyes we will also occasionally see ourselves at our worst. For one who is unprepared, who has let down all defenses without any awareness of the double-edged nature of true insight, the horror of this experience may endanger the mind.

Paul and Jeanne gambled everything on each other. They held back no pieces of themselves; that's love, and it gets scary. Blind as we are to our own faults always, I don't recognize the shadow that crosses your brow for what it is: the reflection of my own carelessness. Instead I start to think that *you* don't care, and paradoxically that makes me angry.

Love is Seeing. But Seeing is a struggle, it's real hard work. Something in us resists, always. So love becomes a fight.

Oh no, it can't be so. Paul was nineteen, he didn't understand. Jeanne was twenty-eight, she didn't understand either (who among us does? no one mortal) but she knew from experience what was happening. Deep in love but running scared, five weeks into this impossibly intense and increasingly rocky relationship, she decided to cover her bets. Unconsciously, perhaps. Consciously, she just found herself attracted to another man.

Paul grabbed hold: I won't let you go, was all he could think. He meant: I'm sorry. I love you. I'll try harder. But the only way he could say it was, YOU CAN'T LEAVE ME. It was too late, but he held tight anyway, and finally to get free of this insane grip she blasted him full force with the hate-side of what he looked like to his loved one. Meanwhile he was dishing it out just as hard as she was. Both of them were badly hurt in the explosion.

Living together. Privacy is at the heart of so many human conflicts, but we seldom recognize it. In estimating our own capacities to achieve miracles, we are often most foolishly generous in calculating the amount of privacy we can live without. Intimacy is indeed the high point and fulfillment of most human friendships and love relationships. But you can't have it every minute, every night, every week, or ever for sure. It's too special: the energy isn't always there. If you force it to be there, you (eventually) burn out the system. And if you just pretend that it's there — go through the motions of intimacy — you commit a terrible invasion of your own and the other's privacy which finally is impossible to bear or forgive.

Paul and Jeanne were living together in the sense that her Greenwich Street apartment (remind me to tell you what happened to that apartment) was literally around the corner from Paul's place on Jane Street; they spent almost all their free time together at one apartment or the other every night from the moment they first got together (making love to each other that summer night; the moment of union) until the time six weeks later (eternal six weeks, a lifetime) when their love finally collapsed of its own weight. They were living together, something Paul had never done before, and at the same time they were working together in the absolute tension of an unstructured situation compounded by debts and deadlines. Their sexual life was magnificent — nineteen-year-old boy has great capacity and enthusiasm, twenty-eight-year-old woman has a mature sense of her own body, and when both are intensely beautiful and sexual in each other's eyes it's an incredible combination — and they shared an intimacy beyond sex, talking and talking, total sharing of each other's present and past, the playground of the mind where the child in you and the child in me go off to play together with full adult awareness, laughing, hand in hand.

Paul-and-Jeanne was doomed from the start, and a great success — a major event in Paul's story.

Sex. Love. Do we see each other? What do we see, that gets us so excited? In August 1967, my buddy Paul spent a lifetime with a woman named Jeanne, and when it ended he thought his life was over. He went around shoving his hand through windows. She got her insides all twisted, had to go to the hospital. They weren't good for each other. But the time they had together was a miracle, and no one would dare to regret it, ever. Paul got over his heartbreak, he walked close to the edge for a while but when he got himself together again you couldn't help noticing he'd grown a lot. Adolescents grow fast, it's exciting to see them in action. And terrifying.

We live with others half-consciously at best. Privacy is invaded more often than love is made. And we really don't know what we're doing. But by taking the risk, we get into realms of reality unreachable through any other door.

Sexual love gets us in trouble. There is nothing more foolish, or more noble. Love is the road to Knowledge.

XV.

In a way I suppose I'm looking for my heart in my past in this book, which is a paradox since heart is always here and now. But really, as I've said before, what I'm examining is the fact of memory, the past that exists in the present.

The past is in the present every day. I hear it on the radio, I smell it in the air. I perceive in context of past perceptions. I am nobody, but my past lets me masquerade as somebody, which is how we get through the day.

Heart is a muscle. It tightens and relaxes, it goes and goes and eventually it stops. I carry a CPR card. A woman once told me she was attracted to me by my heartbeat. If the heart stops, does time stop? Yes and no.

Time stops and keeps going. I don't know

how to explain it. I die — I stop, and yet at the same moment I keep going in all those other places I am, the people who know me, my ripples on the surface of the pond.

I am dead and I am not dead. I could be Paul speaking these words, I don't have to be Don, we are both the same person, we share the same experience. Not the memories. What we share is the experience itself.

In fact, I am not Don, if you judge identity by memories. I, the "I" writing this book, do not have Don's memories. I do have (reasonable access to) Paul's memories. But —

But I am Don's consciousness; and I am also Paul's; and I tell you I feel as one person. Open your heart, you, and you may also find that you are more people than you think.

Don McNeill's loft-apartment on Bleecker Street. Yes, I can picture it clear as day, clear as the dimly lit beauty and holiness of two friends at two a.m. in the dust of a New York apartment, shining in that special privacy like two lights in the golden eternity.

At one time it was a shop to repair industrial sewing machines. Now Don was subletting from the artist upstairs, sharing his front room with a lot of filled and empty canvases. He got to live in the other part of that front room, plus a bedroom that doubled as hallway, and a cave-like

                                      Paul Williams

kitchen. There was a tiny bathroom off the bedroom, with a tile floor, a place where I experienced unforgettable and indescribable visions.

I remember Don as being in his bathrobe a lot — I don't notice clothes much, so I'm not sure this impression is literally accurate, but that's what it felt like — he was always getting up from a nap, always brewing coffee and forever asking me if I'd like a cup, not remembering from one hour to the next that I didn't drink coffee, or remembering the instant he asked, like he forgot but then remembered, but asking me anyway just in case I'd changed my mind. Don was polite to an absurd degree, but a very deep and sincere politeness, innate Buddhism, he had the air of a soul who's been around for millions of years and has been truly humbled by the experience.

His gentleness was extraordinary, and it was totally natural. There hasn't been anyone else like him in my life — each friend is different, of course, but no one has ever made me feel that comfortable that consistently. His note was exquisite.

I hear that note now, picturing Don's loft, "Are you *sure* you wouldn't like some coffee?", with that wonderful open-faced question of a smile. I feel it, and I smile in response.

"Yes, Don, I'll have that coffee now." (big smile from him, fumbling to wash out a cup: "I knew you'd come around eventually.")

Oh, awkward story. Thinking about my past and writing about it are two different things, I wish I could turn it all into fiction but that device won't work for me. I'm lucky to have Don's help with this sometimes but still it doesn't come easy.

Don went to Alaska. We lost touch with each other somewhat when I got so wrapped up in Jeanne, so my memory's not too clear just when it was but the lease was up on his Bleecker Street loft, he stored his things & got a haircut and went to visit his family in Juneau. He was gone for months, seeing friends in Seattle, checking out the scene in San Francisco. Sometime in November I went west myself, it was all over between Jeanne and me and I'd come through the worst of my subsequent craziness, but we were still working in the same office, it wasn't easy and I felt like travelling anyway, as soon as I could I turned over the reins of the magazine for a month and headed for California.

Don and I passed each other, he got back to Manhattan a few days after I left. And he needed an apartment, so he answered an ad in the *Voice* (as an employee

he got a jump of a few hours on all the
other apartment hunters waiting for the
paper to come out) and rented the first
apartment he looked at. It was a studio (one
room) in a recently rebuilt building on
Greenwich Street in the West Village. It was
the very apartment where I'd become so
thoroughly entangled with Jeanne — she
was the one who'd placed the ad that Don
blindly and unerringly answered — she was
moving out to move in with her new lover,
in Brooklyn. I came back (I'd left my apartment too, I didn't live around the corner
any longer, when I got back to town I moved
into a dormitory managed by a friend of
mine, up on 168th Street) and found myself
hanging out in the same familiar apartment,
with the same graffito on the wall even, but
a totally different place now that it was Don
instead of Jeanne who lived there. (The graffito was something I'd written towards the
end of an acid trip with Jeanne; it was on
the wall above the bed, and said, "*Indefinite
Pronoun*, a novel by the great Paul Williams."
Every artist sooner or later tries to put his
signature on the whole thing, isn't that so?
The hard part is finding the lower right
hand corner . . .)

   January 1968 seems so far in my memory from July 1967; the transition from
Don's Bleecker Street loft to Don's Greenwich

Street apartment (by way of Jeanne's Greenwich Street apartment) was a big one for
me, maybe for him too. But I'm not going to
say anything more about it right now.
Instead I'm going to leave you with the last
two paragraphs of Don's rap that opened
this chapter, which I've been saving in case
I needed them now:

I am dead and I am not dead. You don't
believe me; you don't understand. You think it's
got to be one or the other. You think in terms of
black and white: he is either here or he's not here.
And yet we are all of us only partially here every
beating moment of our lives.
We are only partially here, even as our hearts
beat steadily. And when they stop beating, we are
only partially gone.

XVI.

These words must perhaps be more coura-
geous and adventurous than they have been.
What I am reaching for still eludes me, which
suggests I must reach further, and more bold-
ly. I am concerned with what sort of person
I think I am, I am intrigued with the notion
that those who are dead live on and remain
conscious in the hearts and minds of the
living. But to some extent I feel myself
going in circles as I touch on these matters,
and that is because they are so hard to
integrate with this other mystery which has
such a different flavor, the movie of my
past, this apparent succession of events
and impressions which fills my mind when I
consider the fact of my life. Am I alive in

the things I've done, the people I've touched,
the music I've heard — or only in the spark
that leaps this very moment as I stand before you, before myself, dancing till the sun
is gone? Time is mystery, & the accumula-
tion of time, our life stories, the lines of
character in our hands or in our faces, these
are manifestations that promise satisfaction, I want to touch and embrace them and
feel whole. So I sit down and write about
my past like little exercises in describing
reality, very clumsy exercises I admit but
these are steps I have to try to take, my
heart wants something that lies due east on
the other side of this water.

My heart wants breakthrough.
Among Don McNeill's papers, after he died,
I found this phrase: "We're on the verge of a
nervous breakthrough." Okay. Trembling on
the edge, beyond exhaustion, there is a
moment of bliss. When we push too far, and
then go past that, this is what we're pushing for. Suddenly the body feels light, you
feel you could be blown away like a feather.
If only — Okay. I know you want it. But I
can't tell you the secret.

The secret is not to know. We have to
pass from unconscious to conscious and
then on to unconscious again. There is
always a greater mystery. We grow up but
we don't reach maturity. Because that's a

place to stop. And the only truth is keep
going.

And only not to know keeps us going.

But it doesn't matter. The heart doesn't
care. Heart is a wish, a desire. Stand on
your head, my friend. Don't you understand
by now?

Perhaps what I like best about the
music I've grown up with (by which I mean
specifically Bob Dylan, The Velvet Underground, Neil Young, The Beach Boys, The
Rolling Stones) is that (again and again) it
satisfies my need for new language. I have
to hear new language. Finally I have to
think new language. Everything else makes
me crazy.

My heart wants something. I'm going to
make this my private book, I don't see any
reason not to. I need the language, I don't
care about the story any more. Of course I
care about the story. But it gets so narrow.
Am I an entertainer? Then allow me to play
the fool.

It's a dream. It's one of those dreams
where your kid comes in and wakes you up
in the morning, and you go back to sleep
and into the same dream again, this happens a half-dozen times and still the same
story, same cast of characters, that's what it
feels like anyway. And it's not hard to tell,
at least at first, which is the reality and

which is the interruption.

What am I reaching for? I want to find something new inside myself, I don't want to get stuck with the job of repeating what I've already said (no matter how loud the applause). I wake up to find myself driving this automobile down the highway at sixty miles an hour, everything's under control and I'm moving right along but what am I doing here? Turn on the radio and they're talking about the traffic. That's me, I'm the traffic — and it seems kind of silly, to have come this far just to be one of 2000 other people who are tying up the approaches to the Golden Gate Bridge, or one of two million who have made Fleetwood Mac double platinum. The question is not whether I'm unique. I know that as well as any snowflake. Perhaps I'd like to convince myself of the power of my own uniqueness, that the world can't turn without me, which has got to be true because I'm here and the world is turning. All acts and beings are interconnected and indivisible, right? Have you noticed that, how it's all a single piece? All right, then let's talk about it. Let's talk about the way one person reaches out to another person. What is the promise that makes us go to such lengths to show we're attracted to each other? Sexual fulfillment? Animal need doesn't explain the perplexities of

                    Paul Williams

love. It's a larger dance than that, at moments of true perception we see every detail is just as it has to be, truly joyous the hand of God moving each crumpled piece of paper down the street. And doesn't Jimmy Carter doubt his Lord for just a moment, as he grimaces Bert Lance goodbye and turns to face the loneliness? Why separate friends? Why make the job even harder than it has to be? None of us knows, and true doubt is a profound luxury only the faithful can understand. To know that none of this is here — it's all done with mirrors, just a shimmering dream — and then to have to deal with every bit of it at face value all the more so as the price of that knowledge, that's the test, that's the big Zen joke, all of this is just illusion & so be aware of every pore on the illusion's face if you ever want to taste true freedom.

What am I reaching for? I'm reaching for new language. I want to go beyond my own expectations, and it isn't easy. I want to see. I want to see myself, I want to tell you about every moment in which I've seen something that made me feel special, recently I've dreamed of writing a whole book taking off from Bob Dylan's 1976 live album *Hard Rain*, because the contradiction between what I hear in that record (it's one of his best, an album-of-the-moment that

transcends and adds onto everything that's
come before) and the hostile or indifferent
attitudes of most everyone I've talked to
about it, this contradiction seems to me to
go right to the heart of who-we-are in the
1970's. We've gone past the Tower of Babel,
and we don't ever realize that what's holding us apart is we've all started speaking
different languages. Which isn't bad. What's
bad is when even Bob Dylan, who has hun-
dreds of thousands of avid & intelligent
followers, goes unheard, unheard *because*
he's speaking new truths, *because* he's cutting new paths with every bit of the intensity he had in the good old days, and his
audience who were growing so fast along
with him back then now cling desperately
to the old truths and old language still
ringing in their ears, going slowly deaf to
new reality just like the generation they
rebelled against and shit they don't even
know it. And more than that, because what I
want to say taking off from *Hard Rain* is
really very positive: listen to how alive this
guy is on the eve of his thirty-fifth birthday,
the message is loud and clear, this is just
the beginning! There's a second wind, and a
third one behind it, no need to hang back,
let's go out and breathe fire into every cubic
inch of this outrageous universe!

I am a real person. This is the important information, this is what I'm trying to tell myself, this is what I want to get across in this book so every one of us can feel it. Of course we're scared of mirrors! The distance between me in here behind these eyes, and that image of me as seen from outside, is quite simply the largest distance there is — death is nothing compared with the gulf between inside and outside, and that chasm is what we see when we open ourselves to reflection.

And the *only* comfort lies in accepting this awareness, and looking around to realize that others are grappling with it too.

We are all real people. I guess what I'm reaching for, as always, is the courage to proclaim my own existence.

part three

XVII.

Heart of gold in the middle of the air.
Ribbon of sunset in the middle of the night.
I wrote these two sentences on a notepad
on the train with Bear and Chester, two
months ago, rushing across the American
South. How quickly it all becomes the past!
You know I'm right here in the garage (my
office) of the house I live in, and I feel so
homesick it's ridiculous. And shy, like I
don't really want to speak my heart to anyone. But I've decided to force myself to try.

We are alive. We are buried in life with
so many of our own kind all around us and
so much happening at every moment it's
dangerous even to think about it. I'm thinking right now of the people I've talked to in

the last two days and the little things
they've told me about their lives. And what
do *I* ever think about but my own life,
either details of it or what the hell is it all
about anyway? Even knowing lots of good
answers I keep asking, I need to know more.

I need more and it's all so fine just the
way it is I can hardly stand it.

It is now more than three years since I
started writing this book (and I had been
thinking of it for some years before that).
I feel at this time a need to say something
about the current situation. It is a paradox
of this particular project that it claims to be
about the past when any work can only be
about the present. If I were disciplined I
would go ahead and write about the past,
thus allowing myself to speak in the sim-
plest and most open way about exactly
what I feel right now. But a) I am not disciplined, that is the essence of my technique;
and b) I am afraid to speak too openly and
so I hesitate to write. And the only way I
have ever found around this is to turn directly to the issue at hand.

The issue at hand is my anxiety. It's
driving me nuts. The issue is my silence.
It's making me lonely. The issue is my need
to make some progress on this book so I
can get at least the first parts of it out of
my house and into the world. The only

                               Paul Williams

thing I can think of is an act of will: start talking. Start talking and try to tell the truth and don't look back till the job is done. And don't worry about the expectations you can't fulfill. Because in the end you'll be known for the love you gave, and not what you withheld.

Don McNeill and I had a long talk about this book in a coffee shop on Seventh Avenue, not too far from Sheridan Square. It was sometime early in 1968. We decided that books, like people, are just the accidental products of desire. I'm sure it's true of everything. We shook hands and promised never to lose the will to love.

I'm just going to be Paul Williams in this section: we both agreed it would be easier this way. Actually it doesn't matter. Nothing we say can change the truth; and the truth is I will never again be just one person. Two much has happened to turn back now.

According to me I want to write a book. This one, of course, but also another one. A few pages back and a year ago I said I wanted to write a whole book taking off from Dylan's *Hard Rain*. That hasn't changed (one of the things that does allow me to occasionally eventually get things done is the surprising persistence of some

of my desires) but since it also hasn't happened I have at the brief moment (few
nights ago, notes on a scrap of paper) a new
conception of the other book I want to
write, apart from this one which I'm not
writing and the one for money which awaits
a contract. The new conception is a book or
booklet of four essays, on the following
subjects:

> Sturgeon & Psychopaths
> Dylan in the '70s
> Heinlein at Big Mac
> friends and lovers

with the essays written just for the book so
as not to get confused with the needs of
some magazine or newspaper or private
newsletter or whatever.

Okay, it's a nice idea, but let's look at
the actual situation: right now I'm supposed
to be working on an introduction to the
Gregg Press edition of Theodore Sturgeon's
novel *The Dreaming Jewels*. I have a deadline to meet, a tape to transcribe, piles of
notes that just could be fascinating insights
if only I'd sit down and write them up. And
as soon as that's done I've also pretty much
promised to write one for Robert Heinlein's
troublesome *I Will Fear No Evil*. Why dream
up other essays to write (2 of 'em drawing

                    Paul Williams

from the same material) when I've got these obligations/opportunities just sitting in front of me? One would almost suspect it's avoidance.

And there are all sorts of other exciting creative projects that I'm smack in the middle of and deeply committed to — editing four different people's books-in-progress, trying to bring into existence the publishing network that will make public these four books, and two others the manuscripts of which are already complete, and two more we've already printed — plus the major ongoing creative challenge of marriage, children, lovers and friendships. And a few odds and ends I haven't mentioned. This kid has gotten in deep.

So why am I sitting around thinking about new books and essays I want to write when there's all this other stuff demanding my attention? I'm not really sure but I believe the answer is there's something inside of me trying to get out, and what it is is my need to talk on paper. It can be put aside for just so long, and then no matter what else is happening it gets pushy, it gets very insistent, it makes me start acting weird to my wife and friends, makes me unable to focus on my work, this week I think it's given me a sinus infection. Or look at it the other way round, if you like: a certain kind

of writing is therapeutic for me, it's the cure
for the symptoms I've mentioned, and until
I get down to it I'll go on acting weird, blow-
ing my nose etc —

I don't know if these manifestations of
anxiety really stem from my need to write
or from seven other marvelous sources (the
influence of Saturn, a vitamin deficiency,
sexual obsession etc etc) but it doesn't
really matter as long as the cure is to talk it
out . . . and assuming I take the cure. And
that's what I'm leading up to. I'm going to
try to talk about all the different things that
are going on with me, and rap on all the
different subjects I feel a need to expound
on, right here in the pages of *Heart of Gold*.
While still hopefully hanging on to the
original concept of the book — the one that
even precedes or takes precedence over the
idea of writing about my past — which is
the notion of a book that expresses what I
feel in my heart & not just what's on my
mind.

Before, I had to suppress my mind,
even let my beloved departed pal speak for
me, in order to give my heart a chance to
show through. Now it seems I need an opposite approach, got to let my mind run
free & just babble all over if I hope to free
my heart from its shell-shocked shyness
and start speaking my feelings again.

Paul Williams

I feel a need to talk to you. Lately I don't know where to find you. I miss you a lot.

True love is paradise, but paradise is prison. The truth is that courtship is the greatest pleasure in life.

True love is the other side of the bridge. It's so much freedom it scares us shitless.

XVIII.

This body sits at a desk. Answers the telephone. Goes into the house to make a sandwich. Gets on a train and goes to Atlanta, Washington, New York, Chicago. Sometimes someone sees this body and feels affection, feels sexual desire, feels love — it's hard to imagine — but hard to deny. It could only happen because the one body encountered the other body, their space/time coordinates crossed, maybe we went to a party in the same city at the same time, not entirely a coincidence but still when one gets down to the details it inspires a sense of wonder. One love of my life I met because there were too many planes over New York City that morning. We had to spend several extra

hours in the air, we got restless, we started
talking to each other . . . before leaving L. A.
I'd been given the keys to a Manhattan
apartment not far from the East Side Terminal, when the plane finally landed we went
there and as a result our hearts and lives
are still tangled now nine years later . . . her
body is somewhere in Asia at the moment,
India or Bali, she hasn't written, I wish it
were here with mine. This body has work to
do. This body plays solitaire instead of
transcribing interviews, it wants immediate
gratification. This body doesn't like the hot
weather. This body remembers swimming
in the ocean every morning for six months
in Canada eight years ago and feels a long-
ing but stays at home. There's work to be
done and I guess I'm afraid of the ocean.
This body has friends and talks to them but
is never quite satisfied. This body has many
desires. This body needs inspiration. This
body likes to show off for members of the
opposite sex, it's a weakness but it's also a
strength, otherwise surely Dylan's songs
(all the good ones) would never have been
written.

Homesick for what? Homesick for all
those moments going by. Already I feel nos-
talgic about the three of us guys hanging
out on the train together two short months
ago. Mm, not so short really. May/June,

                                    Paul Williams

Atlanta New York Chicago, contained many lifetimes; I still can't hardly think about most of it. And June/July, here in California, has also covered lightyears in its own more centralized way. Life is rich. But never enough. As many times as I've reached enlightenment and all that, still I'm ridden with guilt about the work not accomplished today, and filled with desire for all the possibilities that run through my mind.

Don't tell me to learn to accept. I like things the way they are. I like feeling homesick, it's such a delicious yearning, it's amazing how sloppily one can just be with friends, rolling on some adventure, drinking coffee together at an outside table in the L.A. sun, and then months or years later those moments recollected are the most precious treasure any billionaire could own. Let me breathe deep the aroma of this one, it hurts, it feels so fine.

Heart of gold falls apart, you see. I've been trying to pick up this thread for years now, and it just won't happen, and why? Do I lack the courage my work demands? Or the discipline?

Maybe I lack the incentive.

I fall apart. I fall into open arms of the universe. I like things the way they are. "Man, I just can't tell you, this woman," I wrote in a song, "What she does to me. / I have walked through many a valley / Never felt so free." (An earlier verse says, "I have lived a long, long time / Can't remember when. / I have climbed up many a mountain / Just to get to the bottom again.") That was in 1970. Nothing has changed at all.

This body doesn't really understand. There's too much to do each day to stop and think. Thinking just generates more thinking, anyway. "I want to kiss you all over," as the current hit song proclaims. It's true. This body and this mind and heart work together very closely at times. But *why* — she asks me — do I want to kiss her?

She asks too much.

There are forces at work here. Aren't we fools, finally, to pretend otherwise? The forces want us to love. And we don't care. We go ahead and do it anyway, because it feels so good.

Heart of gold wakes up. This body is dead, it fell into a mirror. This body is alive, so alive you don't know what you're missing not being in bed with me tonight. This body can walk through walls, has seen the glory, has seen the dawn on the highway. This body remembers the music, like it remembers a person it used to be, long ago.

Someday I'll be ready to tell my stories. All the love affairs and the mixed emotions, friendships and changing ambitions,

dreams dreams dreams. It's been fun and
it's just beginning. But now I feel I want this
book on the street, incomplete as it is,
hopelessly untogether — I can't bear to
stick it back in a drawer while more time
passes — let it be incomplete on the street,
let it sell eight copies total, that's okay, I
wanted the eight of you to read it.

Don, do you have anything to say here?

Hi Paul. Look at yourself, but not too often.
Look in the mirror, and see the whole world
standing behind you. Then turn around.

Don't you have some work to do today?
Come see me at midnight, we can talk till
morning.

BOOKS BY PAUL WILLIAMS:

Practical philosophy:

Das Energi
Remember Your Essence
Fear of Truth (*Energi
    Inscriptions*)
Waking Up Together
The Book of Houses (with
    astrologer Robert Cole)
Coming
Nation of Lawyers
Common Sense
*How to Become Fabulously
    Wealthy at Home in
    30 Minutes*

Hippie memoirs:

Time Between
Apple Bay or Life on the Planet
Heart of Gold

Collections:

Pushing Upward
*Right to Pass and Other
    True Stories*

Music:

*Performing Artist, The Music of
    Bob Dylan*, Volumes I & II
*Brian Wilson & the Beach Boys
    —How Deep Is the Ocean?*
Neil Young—Love to Burn
*Rock and Roll: The 100
    Best Singles*
*Watching the River Flow:
    Observations on Bob Dylan's
    Art-in-Progress 1966-1995*
*The Map—Rediscovering Rock
    and Roll*
Outlaw Blues
Back to the Miracle Factory

Other arts:

The 20th Century's Greatest Hits
*Only Apparently Real: The
    World of Philip K. Dick*

Edited by Paul Williams:

*The International Bill of
    Human Rights*
*The Complete Stories of
    Theodore Sturgeon*
(magazines: *Crawdaddy!*
The PKD Society Newsletter)

ALL in print. For a catalog or ordering information, contact:
Entwhistle Books, Box 232517 Encinitas CA 92023 USA
www.cdaddy.com   (look for **Entwhistle Books** button)
phone or fax: 760-753-1815   email: EB@cdaddy.com